REBECCA WEAR ROBINSON

ACTIVIST

IN THE BUSINESS OF CHANGE

CONTENTS

To Sam and Cate, *mes raisons d'être.*

To Jill, the magnitude of change we envision
is possible because of our wide-ranging
conversations.

PREFACE

Ask anyone about drowning and they know someone who has drowned, has had a scare themself, or at least find the prospect terrifying. In the United States, more 1–4-year-olds die by drowning than any other cause.[1] Globally, drowning is the third leading cause of unintentional injury death, with 90% of drownings occurring in low- and middle-income countries.[2] The real drowning rate is likely to be much higher because many countries lack data – countries where we know drowning rates are high. As the climate emergency accelerates, with rising seas and increasingly violent storms and flooding, so will drowning rates. Water covers 70% of the Earth's surface. We cannot live without water for more than three days. The dangers presented by water are inevitable, but the danger of drowning is not inevitable. Drowning occurs not from a lack of awareness, but from the right kind of awareness. If we change how we identify, direct, communicate, teach, and re-inforce safer attitudes and behaviors around water, drowning rates will drop as the new behaviors become as natural as looking both ways to cross the street to avoid being hit by a car.

Drowning is preventable.

It is not just drowning; all social change is directed. No social change is inevitable or accidental. Change always happens. How and whether we choose to direct that change has far-reaching implications. As the t-shirt slogan says, "You can't stop the waves, but you can learn how to surf." Change is directed by whomever has the best vision, strategy, skills, and implementation plan.

This book puts those skills in the hands of activists. It outlines the techniques I have learned to create sustainable, internalized behavioral change. I have integrated the principles of business learned in my B.A. in finance from the University of Illinois and my master's in marketing, economics, and international management from the Kellogg School of Management at Northwestern University. I have applied my natural default system of analysis, bolstered by decades of nonprofit and corporate consulting skills, and rounded it off with a deep understanding of how we change attitudes and behaviors from my master's in organizational and social psychology from the London School of Economics.

My brain is business, but my heart is pure activist. I am in the business of change.

I have been an activist since I was 10 years old. I followed the example of my parents with their lifelong dedication to social justice. My dad was a quiet activist, showing up with his tool kit to repair low-income housing and volunteering in different capacities until the day he died, just shy of his 95th birthday. From my dad, I learned the value of stepping up, sharing my skills, and a generations-deep commitment to service. My mom was a more vocal activist. She had the fire, the anger, and fought for what she believed. From her, I learned to march, write letters, make calls, speak out, advocate for others, the value of community to create change, and that fighting for a better world is important and deeply satisfying.

I have applied the techniques I have learned directly to the drowning prevention field for 15 years, but the techniques are directly transferrable to other areas. Today, we face some of the greatest challenges humanity has ever seen. Climate breakdown. Pandemics and other global health crises. Tension between democracy and autocracy. The sixth mass extinction of species. Violence. Almost constant war. Hate and bigotry in all forms. Cultural division. Misogyny and gender inequality. Staggering wealth disparity, which has created societal unrest and unfairly allocated power.

The magnitude of the necessary changes can seem overwhelming. Unless we create a new paradigm for social change, life will be immeasurably more difficult for most of the world's population.

Eight years ago, I wrote a proposal on how to end drowning. The original plan was idealistic and naive, with only lashings of pragmatism. In the early days, I fell prey to the "if you build it, they will come" delusion. It seemed so obvious. How hard could it be to solve a problem where everyone is at risk and simple behavioral change is the answer? Drowning is an epidemic. (Data confirms the problem.) People want to live; parents love their children and want to keep them safe and alive. (Tap into emotion with awareness campaigns.) Connect with skills-based training. (Change behavior.)

I built it. They did not come.

I passed through the stages of grief. Denial, anger, bargaining, depression, and finally acceptance. This book is, in part, the outcome of my analysis of why they did not come, and the lessons that can be applied to all social change fields where change in attitudes and behaviors is required. My goal is to fast-track activists past common barriers to success.

Technically, I failed. I implemented only one small portion of my plan. In reality, I succeeded beyond my expectations. By trial and error, I developed a far deeper understanding of how to create social change and incorporated what I learned as a member of the steering committee tasked with creating the first U.S. National Water Safety Action Plan, an action recommended by the World

Health Organization.[3] I was also a member of the Water Safety Taskforce Metro Chicago, co-authoring the city's first water safety plan.[4] I pivoted. I adapted. I looked at what worked and what I needed to do differently. I learned. This book encompasses what I have learned about strategically and efficiently pulling together effective methods from a range of disciplines to create sustainable social change.

The global drowning prevention field was my hands-on laboratory, but the techniques I used can be applied to every area of social change. In fact, my strengths and impact in the drowning prevention field came specifically from *not* being an expert in drowning prevention, but instead in social psychology, marketing, and business. I was able to see existing challenges with fresh eyes while listening, asking questions, analyzing, and gaining a deep understanding of the issues from established subject matter experts. Drowning prevention is underfunded, a risk to every person on the planet, and is staffed by a small but passionately engaged group of people, and behavioral change is the primary solution. It provides the ideal topic for a case study on an innovative new approach to cost-effective, sustainable, and internalized social change.

This book is for people who want to change the world. It is for activists. It is for organizations of all sizes. It is for visionaries and pragmatic realists. It is for anyone who is passionate about positive change but frustrated at the glacial pace of change. This book outlines the fundamentals of social change and teaches us how to tackle big problems and get measurable, sustainable results.

Chapter 1

PEEL BACK
THE LAYERS

*Those of us who love peace must organize as effectively
as the war hawks. As they spread the propaganda of war we
must spread the propaganda of peace.*

Martin Luther King Jr.[5]

December 26, 2004. More than a quarter of a million people died when a tsunami slammed into Asia. Around 80% of the victims were women and children. They couldn't swim. They never had a chance. Water was to be feared, and the strategy was to stay away from the water. No one had a plan for the water coming to them.

Some 8,000 miles away, Christina Fonfé watched the destruction unfold with horror. A British nurse and military wife, Christina announced, "I have to do something," connected with an organization already in place, and boarded a plane to Sri Lanka. She intended to use her nursing skills, but there were few survivors requiring medical attention. Christina pivoted. She began to look for the underlying causes.

The first step in addressing any issue, no matter how large or small, is to look at the big picture, and then peel back the layers to find the underlying causes and identify which behavioral changes will make a difference. There are nuances to behavior change that I will cover in Chapter 10, but for the sake of simplicity, I will use the word "behavior" throughout the book since the end goal should always be sustainable behavior change.

If I bombard you with highly emotional messages telling you that it is your responsibility to save humanity, your brain begins a complex reaction, drawing on emotional flight-or-fight instincts while factoring in all you have learned. Your adaptive brain works to balance and connect huge amounts of data. Human brains have evolved into the marvelously complex, logical, and intellectual miracles that make it possible for us to solve huge challenges, have relationships, and feel the full range of emotions.[6] However, we are heavily influenced by emotion as much, or even more so, than logic.[7] When we are overexposed to constant emergencies or overwhelming obstacles, the emotional flight-or-fight response seems like a good option. Logic and nuance are out the window.

Stepping back from the emotional intensity of any issue and putting it into perspective is the first step. Local, national, or global, start by peeling back the layers to identify all the contributing factors and root causes. When I coach people on big projects, my recurring reminder is, "How does a crab eat a whale? One bite at a time." (True: when a whale dies, it sinks to the bottom of the ocean, and over time, one bite at a time, it disappears.) Effective activists adopt the same approach when tackling big changes. They confront the issue one bite at a time. They identify solutions that make a difference and result in sustainable behavioral change. Not only does this technique get to the root of the problem, so that an effective strategy can be developed and implemented, but it also calms the reptilian brain from reacting to negative influences. It derails the competition by not letting them manipulate you.

After peeling back the first layer, Christina's next response to the crisis was to directly address the cultural fear of water and teach women to swim and survive in the ocean. As a qualified swim instructor, she focused on using her specific expertise to make a difference. Over time, Christina learned that focusing on teenage girls, the future mothers, had the strongest impact in the community.

As with any change, there were barriers. It took some time to identify a location, instructors, and swim attire that conformed with cultural norms about gender and modesty – another layer peeled back. One student uncovered a layer that Christina had never anticipated. Saanvi (not her real name) was known to be a talented athlete, but her first lesson was a disaster. She assumed her athletic skills would translate to the pool, but she could not float or even keep her balance standing in the pool. Embarrassed, she retreated to her home, intending never to return. Christina saw Saanvi's potential and lured her back into the water with the promise of the coveted free swimsuit. Within days, Saanvi was swimming and teaching other students what she had learned.

Christina learned that Saanvi struggled in school due to undiagnosed dyslexia. Outside the pool, Christina worked with Saanvi to qualify her as a swim instructor by arranging for the manuals and examination papers to be translated into the local language. Saanvi was able to answer exam questions verbally and her answers were written down for her, thereby bypassing the barriers posed by dyslexia. Five years later, she was fluent in English, teaching swimming, and managing 14 male swimming instructors in a major city. Later, she taught internationally, earning an even higher salary. Saanvi helped to support her family financially and was viewed with pride by her family, school, and community. Her experience encouraged local schools to understand dyslexia and adapt their approach, helping to make teaching swimming an acceptable and safe form of employment for women. It was not just the young women who benefitted from Christina's first big idea and commitment to peeling back the layers; the entire community developed a better understanding of the water and learned how to manage the risks around water, how to recognize and handle dyslexia, and how to create new opportunities for women.

Follow wherever the data and experiences take you, even when they seem to divert from the big idea. You don't have to solve all the problems yourself, but when you understand how the pieces fit together, you can identify collaborators and form partnerships that spread the costs and increase the impact. You begin to shift change on a big level.

What you find when you look beyond the surface never fails to fascinate me. Reality rarely matches our assumptions. In my master's thesis, I looked at why professional women were leaving corporate jobs. The conventional wisdom was that women just didn't want to work, or it made economic sense to stay home with children. But as I dug into the issue, it became clear that women wanted to redefine how the work was done; not just flexibility in start times but a much broader rethinking that encompassed how women think and interact when solving problems, creating, and rethinking processes and outcomes. This was in 2000. Fast forward to 2020, and the COVID-19 pandemic forcibly peeled back the layers about how work is done for everyone.

So many fascinating and often simple solutions to complex problems can be identified when you look beyond the obvious. Girls missing school? Supply feminine hygiene products when girls are menstruating. Sexual violence in public toilets in a slum in Cape Town, South Africa? Hire local women to clean and manage the toilets, paid for by a small usage fee. Decrease drowning deaths among boaters? Install life jacket loaner stations on public boat docks. We can apply the technique to overwhelmingly large issues as well. Wealth inequality is a root cause and misogyny is a strong contributing factor in our failure to address the climate breakdown. (Some 50% of carbon emissions come from the top 10% of wealthy people, and 88% of billionaires are male.[8]) Drowning in the United States and many other countries has roots in the forcible disconnection of Indigenous and minority populations from skills derived from cultural heritage. This historical disconnection is a direct contributing factor to higher drowning rates in those populations.

Look at the data. Talk to people. What's working? What's not working? What are the root causes of the problem? Keep asking why until you get to the "aha" moment. The technique comes from Toyota engineer Taiichi Ohno's famous Five Whys systemic problem-solving tool, designed to figure out the true problems, not just the surface symptoms. Start by looking at existing behavior and asking the question, why? Break down the answer and ask again, why? Ask until you have asked the question why five times. It may take more or less than five whys, but following the why train is a simple but effective way of getting to the crux of the matter.

For instance, to address drowning in the United States, we need to understand where people drown and whether certain groups are at higher risk. So, we begin to break down the issue using data and then further break it down using the five whys. One data stream shows us that Black children drown at almost three times the rate of white children. Black children aged between 10 and 14 drown in swimming pools at a rate 7.6 times higher than for white children.[9]

1. Why? Because fewer Black children learn to swim.
2. Why? Because there is a cultural bias against learning to swim.
3. Why? Because prior to the enslavement of Africans and African Americans, Africans were viewed as superior watermen and the best swimmers in the world. They were sought after on sailing ships because of their swimming skills. This skill in the water, which was often not possessed by their white owners and overseers, allowed slaves to escape by

swimming across lakes and rivers to freedom. White slave owners retaliated by refusing to let slaves learn to swim. Once slavery ended, Jim Crow laws created a segregated society which excluded Black people from beaches and swimming pools and resulted in fewer Blacks learning to swim and pools being closed in predominately Black neighborhoods. Widely discredited research used to perpetuate racist stereotypes declared that Black people are more likely to sink due to their heavier bones (not true), but which became "fact" to both Blacks and whites.[10]

Using the whys shows us which issues need to be addressed. Asking why exposes entrenched racism, belief systems, and barriers to learning to swim as underlying issues. Without addressing these issues, we have little chance of lowering drowning rates among the Black population. This reality was reinforced when I participated in focus groups about water safety in Chicago in November 2020. The race riots of 1919 stemmed from segregated access to Lake Michigan. Racism and a cultural resistance to swimming remain entwined in attitudes about swimming and equal access to pools to this day. It should be noted that data confirm that access to public pools is currently equal across the city, so equitable progress has been made, but private pools are predominately in affluent white areas, reinforcing both the perception and reality that Black people are still denied equal access to pools for swimming lessons and recreation. Keep peeling back the layers.

Make asking why an intentional exercise, one that is regularly repeated at least quarterly. Every time you hit a roadblock, repeat the exercise. Every time you are evaluating partnerships, collaborations, or identified new competitors, ask why? Use a whiteboard, shareable document, pen and paper, whatever approach works for you and your team, but write it out. Treat the results as a historical document, one you can reference when your strategy isn't working as planned, or when you have achieved your first goal and are ready for the next step. Change never stops, new variables always pop up, and people aren't always predictable. When activists assume the job is done, the competition sneaks in and redirects the change. Every single time.

Critically, the process of peeling back the layers also exposes the underlying emotions that people feel, the emotions that influence how we behave. We are far more influenced by our emotions than by logic. As the neuroscientist Jill Bolte Taylor said, "Although many of us think of ourselves as thinking creatures who feel, biologically we are really feeling creatures who think."[11] Without understanding and engaging emotion, directing social change is challenging, if not impossible.

We resist the idea that our emotions are vulnerable and susceptible. Even talking about engaging emotions for change can feel like manipulation, but it isn't the normal human engagement of emotions that is good or bad, it is the intent. Engaging emotions can radicalize with the intent of hatred and aggression, as we have seen with violence against racial, religious, and LGBTQ+ groups. Emotions can also mobilize movements such as #MeToo and #BlackLivesMatter, raise funding for cancer research, encourage people to embrace green energy, and pass legislation. Emotions are every bit as involved in the local school board election as they are in national elections.

The business world understands the necessity of engaging emotions to sell ideas, goods, and services. Always on the lookout for effective strategies, business drew on theories in social psychology to create the discipline of marketing. Marketing is all about understanding and leveraging emotions to change behavior. When you choose between Coke and Pepsi for your drink, or Nike and Adidas for your shoes, your behavior is being influenced by effective marketing campaigns. We accept that marketing is a powerful tool of business. We are even happy that marketing is a powerful tool because, done well, it makes us feel better, stronger, more powerful, and connected. Marketing taps into our emotions in a way that makes us want to engage in the behavior change.

But marketing has a marketing problem among activists. It has been lumped in with all that has caused societal problems in the first place, and then dismissed. We waste time and energy fighting against existing models instead of visualizing and creating a radically new model for the social good. We focus on running away from a bad situation rather than stopping, thinking about what we want, and moving intentionally forward using the most effective tools. It is time to repurpose the tools from other fields, just as business created marketing out of theories from social psychology. Marketing can be used ethically and effectively. Understand how the competition is using marketing to discourage positive change and then turn around and use marketing to launch a counteroffensive. Fight fire with fire.

Social marketing for activists is broader and more powerful than the marketing techniques used to sell soda and shoes. Social marketing pulls what works effectively from marketing and social psychology to create a better world for most of the population.

Social psychology looks at how people relate, individually and within groups, across cultural, geographic, racial, and religious differences. It explores where beliefs come from and how these beliefs make people act. It makes sense that if we understand why people act the way they do, we are in a better position to convince them to change their behavior. Where we have been less successful is in intentionally and strategically using this knowledge to direct positive and sustainable behavioral change for the public good.

Marketing focuses on changing attitudes and behaviors. We don't feel manipulated or forced when behavior change is marketed effectively. On the contrary, we feel pride and ownership in the change. When marketing is done well, we become convinced that the behavioral change is an integral part of who we are, of what defines us. As consumers, we are defined by our loyalty to Chevy or Ford, Target or Walmart, designer fashions or thrift shopping. We can also be defined by our commitment to reducing our carbon footprint by using renewable energy, using gun locks and gun safes to reduce firearm deaths, or installing four-sided pool fencing to reduce drowning deaths. In summary:

Social psychology = understanding people.
Marketing = convincing people to change behavior.
Social marketing = understanding people and convincing them to change their behavior.

Social marketing empowers us to better understand people *and* convince them to change their behavior. It is easy to confuse social marketing with social media marketing. Social media marketing is a tool – an internet-based social sharing tool for reaching a huge number of people and occasionally mobilizing them into action. Social media marketing is used to sell products and, disturbingly frequently, to radicalize individuals. Social media marketing is only a conduit for spreading information and selling. Social media doesn't identify problems, develop strategies, or implement solutions.

Social media marketing is a waterpark, but social marketing is the Pacific Ocean.

Social marketing is an established discipline that is being used effectively around the world to improve health and safety and address environmental concerns. The concept of social marketing was introduced in 1971 by Philip Kotler and Gerald Zaltman, professors at Northwestern University. They identified the power of applying commercial marketing principles to health, social, and quality-of-life issues.[12] Social marketing is cost-effective. From a financial perspective, it provides a high return on investment (ROI), meaning that for every dollar invested, there are quantifiable financial benefits. A study of high-income countries showed a median ROI of 4.1 ($4.10 saved for every $1 invested) for local public health interventions and a median cost–benefit ratio (CBR) of 10.3. Nationwide public health interventions had even better results: a 27.2 ROI and 17.5 CBR.[13] That's right, for every $1 that government spent on using marketing to improve public health, $27.20 of your taxpayer dollars were saved.

Social marketing works and the principles should be widely used, but social marketing alone isn't powerful enough to address the global challenges we face. Today, we need a complete paradigm shift. It isn't enough to shift from fossil fuels to renewable energy to mitigate the climate breakdown, to teach water safety to confront the threat of rising seas and increasingly violent storms, or to replace forms of consumption. We need a radical shift in how humanity relates to our environment. From issues like production and consumption, to in-depth conversations around rethinking power and wealth distribution and addressing the benefits and dangers posed by artificial intelligence, we have the opportunity to create a different future. We have no choice but to do so rapidly and proactively or the decisions will be made for us. Some 99.9% of the world's scientists are sounding the alarm that if we don't address climate change now, the new status quo will be unpredictable and deadly.[14]

We need a complete paradigm shift in how we view social change. To expand social marketing by appropriating effective disciplines from business; not just marketing, but tried and true strategies from finance, accounting, and economics. For simplicity, I will refer to it as *social change marketing* throughout this book. We need to harness the strategies that created successful companies, which in turn transformed societies, for better or for worse. There is a tendency among activists and those pushing for social change to turn against any and all business-related techniques, as if the techniques were the problem. It is never the techniques; it is the intent and the implementation that can either benefit or cause harm.

For example, cigarettes are effectively marketed and cause 8 million deaths a year in smokers and an additional 1.3 million deaths from secondhand smoke.[15] If my goal is to reduce drowning, I can use the same marketing techniques to encourage the desired behavior of swimming lessons for all children. Recognize the competition to change – cultural, cost, access, and the perception that other extracurricular activities have more value. Market the desirability of teaching children to swim by explaining the problem in language that addresses immediate parental concerns: keeping their child alive and healthy. (In the United States, drowning kills more 1–4-year-olds than anything else. Children under 1 usually drown in the bathtub. Children aged 1–4 usually drown in swimming pools. After age 5, most people drown in open water.) Immediately follow with the solution: learning to swim reduces a child's chance of drowning by 88%.[16]

Similarly, guns are in the middle of a decades-long marketing tug-of-war. Culture wars engage emotion over the interpretation of Second Amendment rights. The emotions evoked are of fear, scarcity, the positive belief that having a gun in the house will keep your family safe, the impression that everyone else has a gun (44% of households have a gun), or that "they" are coming for your guns.[17] To reduce gun deaths, market the statistical reality that your child or another loved one is far more likely to die from the gun you purchased than from a gun used by someone outside the house or family. Emphasize that the vast majority of child and teen gun suicides and unintentional shooting deaths occur at a home (20% of teens considered suicide in the last year). As mental health awareness and suicide prevention awareness continue to increase, this opens the door for conversations about safely storing guns.[18] The research supports the behavior change of storing guns unloaded and locked up, with ammunition stored separately to reduce the chance of unintentional injury. Participating in firearm safety training results in guns being stored safely.

I can hear the outrage now: it isn't enough. This is the attitude that keeps change from happening because the opposition is already using the techniques in this book effectively to block your change. Change never happens instantly. It is always the result of determined pressure built up over time. Social change is like water – it finds every nook and cranny. You don't have to blow up the whole dam, you just need to knock out enough rocks and the force of the water will sweep away the remainder. Think strategically. Think long term. Decide which rocks to dislodge.

Consider an example from corporate finance about finding the right rocks (changes) to dislodge. Economies of scale refers to the cost advantage experienced by a firm when it increases its level of output. In simple language, it is cheaper to produce one thousand cars than it is to produce one car, because the time and money must be invested whether you are building one car or one thousand cars. When the cost is spread across more cars, each car is cheaper to produce. With social change, it is more efficient and cost-effective to reach many people than to reach one person. The drowning prevention field in the United States includes many small family foundations with materials, curriculums, and programs that are often produced and distributed locally. They realized that they could benefit from economies of scale and formed an umbrella group, Families United to Prevent Drowning.[19] Each foundation stands alone, but they share stories, program ideas, data, and strategies, making each individual foundation more effective. Equally as important, forming one large group gave them the clout to interact with established national organizations, increasing the effectiveness and reach of all involved.

Change is inevitable. We can either direct the change or be pulled along as others direct it, but change will occur whether we like it or not. Social change can be triggered as a reaction to a cataclysmic event or be a slow-boil creep. Change can be inflicted upon others or adopted joyfully. Social change can be a stated goal or an unexpected outcome. Change can be as seismic as votes for women, the civil rights movement, and the LGBTQ+ rights movement, or as seemingly simple as creating traffic lights and teaching pedestrians to look both ways before crossing the street to cut down on traffic fatalities. Change cannot be contained. Change always has ripple effects, both expected and unintended consequences. For example, the increase of women in the workforce had the unexpected consequence of changing the dress code, which transformed the entire fashion industry. Globalization shifted populations from rural communities to cities in multiple countries, with far-reaching implications for political power, transportation, the climate, wealth distribution, and culture. Globalization also lifted 130,000 people out of poverty every day between 1990 and 2015.[20]

There are seemingly endless examples of damaging change effectively marketed by those who stand to benefit. Aggressive marketing of tobacco, alcohol, sugar, opiates, guns, and fossil fuels distracts from the dangers they pose. The use of hard-hitting and fear-based messaging has pulled us back to the flight-or-fight response with its addictive surge of adrenalin shooting a direct line to our reptilian brain. Fight cancer rather than prevent cancer. Fight poverty rather than prevent poverty. We even fight violence, the ultimate oxymoron. We fight the outcome rather than positively changing attitudes and behaviors that avoid the negative outcomes in the first place. No one would prefer to survive cancer over never getting cancer to begin with.

A potent barrier to change is the ongoing use of fear. Fear makes people easier to control. A wise woman once said to me of her country's long-term dictator, "He's smart – he keeps people just hungry enough and just afraid enough to control, but not so hungry or afraid that they rebel." Harnessing fear takes many forms: threats that our defining cultural, moral, and religious values will be undermined; threats of social ostracism; threats of economic collapse; threats to the stability and safety of the family; threats to the very way of life as we know it. The fear that we will end up at the bottom of the economic, social, and power food chains. Herman Göring, Nazi military leader and convicted war criminal, understood the power of fear. Gustave Gilbert interviewed Göring during the Nuremberg trials and reported that he said, "voice or no voice, the people can always be brought to the bidding of the leaders. That is easy. All you have to do is tell them they are being attacked and denounce the pacifists for lack of patriotism and exposing the country to danger. It works the same way in any country."[21] The quote may or may not be accurate, but we see the use of fear to control in many situations. Whatever your cause, distraction, shame, blame, and fear are all being marketed effectively and pose strong competition to the positive behavioral change you seek.

Potentially, the most damaging aspect of the emphasis on fear is learned helplessness and the sense of powerlessness that arises from a traumatic event or a failure to succeed. It is a slippery slope to deprive a human being of self-determination. It is also deceptively and frighteningly easy to accomplish.

It doesn't have to be this way. We can create true competition to the negative and damaging behaviors that are marketed so effectively. We can reclaim power and direct social change positively. I am not suggesting a total overthrow of existing structures but rather a new paradigm of change using the most effective tools to build a stronger, more stable, and more equitable society. After all, even in the United States, lodged firmly at the "individual rights" end of the spectrum, the Founding Fathers acknowledged that a structure which bound individuals together under a common goal was necessary in the form of the states and the constitution. The human need for structure must be understood and embraced, and the power of these structures harnessed, because the regular calls to break down existing systems are downright dangerous. Not for the frustration they represent but because they are rarely accompanied by a clear vision of an alternative future, backed up by an analysis of the competition and barriers to change and a detailed implementation plan with built-in contingency planning. Nature abhors a vacuum. Without a clear vision and a plan, the better organized competition will always slither in and destroy hard-earned progress.

In upcoming chapters, we are going to create a road map for systematically and effectively changing behavior for the benefit of both the individual and society. No matter what your cause, whether you are focusing on local change or a global movement, this book offers a pragmatic plan to use your existing resources more wisely, efficiently, and cost-effectively.

There are challenges. Destabilizing wealth inequality and the corresponding consolidation of power are at historic levels. Behavior change can transfer power unpredictably. Social media and the explosion of artificial intelligence (AI) was marketed as accelerating the phenomenon of individual empowerment, thereby justifying the lack of regulatory guardrails. Instead, it has further consolidated and shifted wealth and power to a few in the tech industry. Change can be awkward and unearth unexpected consequences, both positive and negative. Corporations, organizations, and governments are averse to change they do not understand or control. As Thomas Dewey reportedly said, "Things that are bad for business are bad for the people who work for business." Many people have a vested interest in continuing to create or treat negative outcomes rather than working to end or prevent those outcomes.

To be successful, positive behavioral changes must pass the cost–benefit test; create desirable jobs; maintain or increase income; decrease healthcare costs while increasing health outcomes; increase quality of life; and protect existing investments in health and welfare, particularly for children. A potentially daunting prospect, but one which I believe can be achieved if we develop a new paradigm for creating positive social change.

This book breaks down the process. There are worksheets at the end of each chapter to help you work through the process. At the end of the book, you will have a solid plan for moving forward. In upcoming chapters, you will learn how to do the following:

- Identify why the underlying problem exists and what behavioral change will produce a different outcome.
- Learn how to wield your unique skills effectively.
- Make others care about your cause using targeted strategies.
- Explore how to harness the power and navigate the role of data.
- Focus on the behavioral change that will make a measurable difference.
- Follow the money to assess the impact on messaging, understand how it fuels the competition, and how budgets dictate change.
- Create key messages which result in the desired behavioral change.
- Lock in the change.
- Understand when the necessary change is in you.

Finally, a word on activists. Activism has been the victim of a negative marketing campaign. It has become a loaded term like "feminism," "liberal," and "conservative." Activism has become synonymous with politics or marching in the street, but it is far more. You don't have to be political to be an activist, but you do have to be an activist if you want a better world for yourself and others. If you care deeply enough about something to fight for it, you are an activist. Often, we don't stop to think about what we value until it is taken away. We become activists unexpectedly. Activism can be as local as saving a nearby wetland, establishing a community garden, or volunteering in a school library. Activism can be national or global, like the events that launched #BlackLivesMatter, #MeToo, #NeverAgain, #FireDrillFridays, and the voter turnout after the Supreme Court overturned *Roe v. Wade*. Activists are anyone who cares enough to speak out or act to make their part of the world a better place. This book is for activists.

Chapter 1 Worksheet

1. Peel back the layers. Keep asking why a problem exists. Keep asking why until you get to the root cause.
2. Don't get distracted by the "how." For now, put the "how," the "who," the "what," and the "where" in a separate document. Capture the information, but don't try to solve or create an implementation plan. We will get to the how in later chapters.
3. What behavior change would solve the why?
4. What have you been conditioned to fight against? For your issue, how often is the word "fight" used? Why are you being asked to fight? Who benefits from continued fighting instead of solving the underlying problem?
5. Identify the ways fear is being used to manipulate your behavior now. Who is doing the manipulating?

WHAT MAKES *YOU* AN EFFECTIVE ACTIVIST?

I am no longer accepting the things I cannot change. I
am changing the things I cannot accept.

Angela Y. Davis[22]

Every single person has what it takes to be an effective activist. We each possess skills necessary to make a significant difference. However, no single person possesses all the skills necessary to solve the big problems. Identifying your unique skills and learning how to use them effectively is power. Identifying partners and collaborators who possess complementary skills amplifies that power. In this chapter, we will explore why it is so important to identify your strengths, how to isolate and name your superpower, and what to do with your unique abilities. We will tackle overcoming our natural bias and how to create the perfect "brain" to make change happen. For this, I respectfully add an addendum to Angela Davis' statement: change the things you cannot accept by harnessing your unique skills effectively and efficiently. Be focused. Be targeted. Be strategic.

When faced with a problem, our natural default is to solve the problem in a way that plays to our strengths. We all know the feeling we get when we are firing on all cylinders, our brain cells are popping, the answers are obvious, and the path forward is clear. We call it the sweet spot or being in the zone. This is the feeling we have when we are leveraging our strengths effectively. Contrast this to being asked to solve a problem in a way that does not play to our skills. Procrastination, resistance, frustration, and feeling like we aren't doing a very good job. It is demoralizing.

Let me give you an example. My long-time best friend is an exceptional community organizer. Her idea of a good time is political canvassing, going door-to-door, and talking to voters. She organizes large events effortlessly and finds meeting with lawmakers enjoyable. The very thought has me running for the hills. The one time I agreed to hand out flyers about a school board election, which involved knocking on the doors of neighbors I had known for years, I fled after the first low-level confrontation, and I am still traumatized. Grassroots community organizing is not my skill. Can I do it? Yes, if I must, but it isn't my primary skill set. I don't enjoy it, and I am not particularly good at it. By contrast, if the assignment is to analyze stacks of research or financial documents, find the patterns and decipher what the data is telling me, and create supporting spreadsheets, time flies and I am dancing a jig as the patterns emerge. Suffice to say, when I mention my idea of fun to my best friend, her eyes glaze over, accompanied by a slight look of panic that she might be asked to participate in the "fun."

Identifying our own skills sounds easy, but we are often blind to our abilities. I see patterns – patterns in data, patterns in numbers, patterns in behavior, patterns in everything – and then I analyze the patterns. It is how my brain works. It is not how most people's brains work. Thank goodness. The world would be one-dimensional if we were all finding and analyzing patterns with Dr. Spock-like intensity. I look at Mozart, Taylor Swift, Van

Gogh, Willa Cather, and Karl Lagerfeld and I am in awe of how their brains see the world, how they create art. So too the engineers working on the Mars rover, surgeons removing tumors from brains, chefs creating new flavor combinations, designers of everything from couture clothing to Apple packaging, teachers of young children, the electrician who can rewire an old house, the builders of stone walls that last for centuries, and my best friend's community organizing skills. I do not possess these skills, but I recognize and value them. More importantly, I know that I am the most effective and productive activist if I partner with people who have different or complementary skills.

Two surefire methods can be used to start identifying your unique skills. First, what comes easily? We tend to discount what comes easily to us, assuming that if it is easy for us, it must be easy for everyone. Nothing could be further from the truth. If it is obvious and easy to you, it is almost certainly one of your core skills. Second, what do others want you to do for them? What task or role are you regularly assigned? What do others look to you to accomplish? These pull on your core skills. Look around your organization, community, family, or even friend group. It is likely that one person is always tagged to organize the events, plan the trips, create the brochures, handle the finances, create a caregiving network, be the healthcare advocate, or come up with a fun uniting activity. Regardless of who declares themself the leader, it is also likely that everyone looks to the natural leader, the person they know will lead effectively in each situation. Those who prefer to follow are at ease and confident carrying out their roles.

Formal tools also exist to identify skills. You may have taken a skills assessment in school. Pull it out again. Chances are some of those skills, even those identified as early as middle school, are still core skills. They just look different under different scenarios. In seventh grade, my skills assessment identified Internal Revenue Service auditor as a perfect career choice. Given that I was painfully shy with a lamentable sausage-roll-curl hairstyle, the idea that I was best suited for a fear-inspiring career was horrifying. (Apologies to IRS agents everywhere. I now realize how cool your work is, although the IRS really needs to market how they benefit society more effectively.) Yet the assessment was correct. What I came to understand over time was that it wasn't necessarily the exact career that the test identified, it was the skill set – the analytical ability coupled with a numerical pattern fluency. They merely matched the skill set to recognized jobs because the purpose was "career aptitude." My community organizer friend matched as a farmer. She can barely grow a house plant and is a dedicated urban dweller, so she also rejected the idea. Looking back, the skills are the same: coordinating a lot of moving parts across a wide community under critical time constraints with attention to individual requirements. Literally growing a movement.

Fads in personal communication style labeling come and go. Early in my consulting career, the Myers–Briggs Type Indicator was used to teach consultants about our preferred style and how to adapt to our client's preferred style. The Myers–Briggs test was first published in 1943 by mother and daughter Katharine Cook Briggs and Isabel Briggs Myers, and was based on Jung's 1921 *Psychological Types*.[23] The validity of the test has been questioned since it was introduced, starting with the fact that the academic community was "unwilling to take seriously the work of two women without graduate degrees."[24] While few women had advanced degrees at that point, Isabel did have significant research and test construction experience and had conducted qualitative and quantitative studies for years. It wouldn't be the first time an original idea by women was dismissed, and it won't be the last, so I am taking the criticism with a pound of salt. Make your own decision. Data is only as good as the interpreter. Take the test online, for free, and see if it rings true.[25] See if it identifies core skills that you know you have or helps you to see your skills in a new light. Personally, I found the test extremely helpful for identifying my core skills and think my picture should be next to INTJ in the promotional materials as a textbook example of the type (highly analytical).

The Birkman Method is another helpful tool for identifying skills. Roger W. Birkman had seen how behavior impacted team performance during the Second World War and went on to create his Test of Social Comprehension in 1951. "The Birkman Method measures various personality traits to provide insights on how they might interact in a team setting."[26] The technique is still used by over 10,000 companies to build effective teams and to improve personal performance, including NASA, numerous health systems, and Intel. I took the Birkman Test shortly after I started working in the drowning prevention field. Highly analytical was again the consistent theme, but the test also gave me feedback on what I needed from team members to feel valued, how to identify what others need to feel valued, and how to strengthen my collaboration skills.

Other approaches include Analytical, Intuitive, Functional, and Personal; Analytical, Driver, Feeler, Influencing; or Passive, Aggressive, Passive-Aggressive, and Assertive.[27] A quick online search produces dozens of other options for identifying skills. According to LinkedIn, 82% of companies use some form of pre-employment assessment test.[28] Fun piece of trivia: the first use of standardized skills tests was in China in AD 605. A nationwide standardized test was devised to select people for government positions – a precursor to today's Foreign Service Officer Test, which vets United States diplomatic candidates.[29] Regardless of the variations, the underlying ideas are the same. Identifying and deploying skills effectively works.

Most of us can comfortably communicate in a range of styles, but we all have a dominant communication style. Identifying your dominant communication style is a tool, not a law, but it is worth the exploration time. For an activist, intentionally and effectively engaging with people who have different communication styles provides a competitive advantage. Working with people who view the world in a different way in order to craft messages and programs which resonate with a range of target audiences gets results. This also applies to engaging with people and organizations in other fields. If there is no discussion or debate, then you have too many like-minded people in the room and are at a competitive disadvantage in the real world.

The final approach for identifying skills is qualitative research, which is a fancy term for asking work colleagues, friends, and family members what they see as your strengths and weaknesses. Some people can identify skills without prompting, but providing them with a list of skills and asking them to circle your top five to ten skills is a simple and effective tool to give you a good overview of how others see you.

Once you have identified your core skills, look at the skills you lack or where you are weak. Finding partners and collaborators who complement and supplement your skills will increase your effectiveness. The intersection of skills to create the best outcome occurs when we take a multifaceted look at an issue. We utilize our individual strengths for maximum impact, but we are stronger working together than as individuals. We are stronger still if we intentionally collaborate with those who have different skills, if we step out of our comfort zone. Combine my analytical skills with my best friend's community organizing skills, and we have exponentially higher chances of success for almost any project.

We tend to gravitate towards people like ourselves or, more accurately, we veer away from people who are different from ourselves. This occurs because of implicit bias, defined by the American Psychological Association as "a negative attitude, of which one is not consciously aware, against a specific social group."[30] We develop these negative attitudes based on our experiences and learned associations. These attitudes can be deceptively simple to defend. As a woman, I will always cross the street if I see a group of drunk or rowdy men because I know from experience that I might be harassed. It feels like common sense, not negative bias that would interfere with my effectiveness as an activist. It becomes implicit bias that will interfere with progress if I flatly refuse to work with any man because of my experiences. We recognize biases related to race, gender, religion, culture, sexual orientation, and socio-economic status. Recognition does not mean that biases are easy to overcome. Bias is easily weaponized to divide and conquer, but seeing the damage bias inflicts can also be the spark that creates activists. The challenge is to combat bias without bias.

We like people like us and are more likely to hire people who remind us of ourselves. This extends to working together as activists within organizations and across movements. We create bias by projecting our positive traits onto someone with a similar background and lived experience, which has a direct impact on how we form partnerships and collaborations, and how decisions are made. This can result in a silo – a small group of people who have common beliefs and interests. Breaking out of the silo requires intentional effort. When I started working in drowning prevention, there were multiple silos within the field. Lifeguards, researchers, swim instructors, and families who had lost loved ones each worked in a silo, but early global conferences identified the problem, and the field responded proactively. Now, there is continuous collaboration between all disciplines working on the issue. The silos have been intentionally dismantled.

The next silo to overcome is to collaborate with other fields. This requires us to peel back the layers of the problem again and step out of the comfort zone of people focused on one issue. Working with climate activists, especially those focused on emergency preparedness, was an example for me of breaking out of the silo and looking at the issue of drowning prevention with fresh eyes. In most countries, racial minorities are at a higher risk of drowning, making racial justice and racial equity activists logical partners. Children who learn to swim have higher IQs, do better in school, and have better physical coordination, making activists focusing on education potential collaborators.[31] It is the idea of building a bigger pie, rather than fighting for crumbs from one small slice of the financial, policy, and program pie. It requires intentionally seeking out those who think differently or whose focus is on a different but complementary issue.

A sure sign that you are in a silo, surrounded by too many people who think exactly like you, is when there is typically broad agreement, answers to problems are "obvious," and others "just don't understand." Groupthink is a concern when there is too much commonality in skills and beliefs. Groupthink is "a phenomenon in which a group of well-intentioned people makes irrational or non-optimal decisions spurred by the urge to conform or the belief that dissent is impossible." It may be "fueled by a particular agenda – or it may be due to group members valuing harmony and coherence above critical thought."[32] In non-academic terms, groupthink is when like-minded people are afraid to disagree or are afraid of being ousted from the group if they speak up. It may feel like peer pressure. This homogeneity in decision-making has broad negative implications. It impacts on which strategies are employed, how priorities are set, and how success is measured. Research shows that when leadership gives the physical appearance of diversity (different races, genders, and backgrounds) but is homogeneously without scruples or unwilling to tolerate dissent, even in the face of overwhelming evidence, the outcomes can be disastrous, even deadly. The *Challenger* Space Shuttle disaster and the Bay of Pigs Invasion are examples of groupthink. In the *Challenger* case, engineers knew there were faulty parts but didn't want negative press. President Kennedy authorized a disastrous clandestine invasion of Cuba but those around him did not speak up because dissent was not encouraged.

Within the realm of activism, lack of diversity in thought and experience results in tunnel vision and silos. For example, if

I surround myself with others who are also deeply analytical, we are in danger of analyzing forever and not converting the analysis into action or conducting analysis that does not take emotions and human impact into account. Worse, the focus on data can ignore the beauty and wonder of the creative arts that makes us human and is a powerful communication tool for engaging emotions to change attitudes and behaviors. As an extreme example, analysis of the breakdown of the climate indicates that the planet and its nonhuman inhabitants would be much better off with no humans – an outcome that is clearly not desirable for humans. In drowning prevention, action-oriented lifeguards who focus solely on rescuing will never make progress on drowning rates without researchers examining which prevention and rescue strategies are effective and educators and communicators translating that research into awareness and education programs. Fishermen in Alaska need different water safety strategies than small children in Florida. Learning to swim in a pool is nothing like being able to swim in the Pacific Ocean. A 2-year-old does not have the same physical and comprehension skills to learn how to swim as a 10-year-old. As the saying goes, it takes a village... Know where your skills fit into the village and advocate for your value to be recognized while actively engaging those with different skills. As renowned Stanford basketball coach Tara VanDerveer says of her leadership team, "Be sure they complement you more than they compliment you."[33]

An unwillingness to sacrifice ideals within a silo in favor of accomplishing the big picture goal is another way we sabotage diversity of thought. At a suicide prevention coalition meeting, one participant walked out because the coordinator misused pronouns. Not intentionally; in fact, the coordinator had apologized profusely, acknowledged the importance of using preferred pronouns, and publicly committed to doing better. While gender-neutral pronouns have been in use since the 14th century, routine usage in daily conversation is fairly recent. The mistake came from decades of habitual use of she/he, not from malicious intent.[34] The data is clear: suicide rates are higher among those who identify as LGBTQ+, so representation from that group is critical on suicide prevention coalitions.[35]

The big picture can be obscured by the details. We divide and conquer ourselves when we don't allow for diversity in thought and life experience and understand that we may have to give a little in the short term to gain substantially in the long term. "My way or the highway" is one of the most damaging mentalities for activists, a fatal off-ramp from solving the big problem. Dividing and conquering is ruthlessly exploited by the opposition. Seeds of doubt are sown. Culture wars are fired up. Think of how often you have heard someone say that they won't vote for a candidate because the entirety of their preferred worldview is not being addressed. In the drowning prevention field, how and at what age swimming is taught to children is hotly contested. Everyone agrees with the big picture – drowning is bad and swimming skills prevent drowning – but teaching infants is hotly contested and divides the field, particularly given the current lack of evaluative research on the various techniques to support or refute people's strong emotions. This division leaves parents confused about what action they should take to protect their child and fragments an already small group of people working on a huge issue.

The advantages of diversity in decision-making have been well documented, particularly in adding gender and racial diversity. Better outcomes, more ethical decisions, less criminal behavior, and more profits. If all our decisions were based on logic, there would be no need for discussions about diversity or the value of recognizing individual strengths and skill sets; it would happen naturally. But we are not rational, we are emotional.

Identifying and intentionally engaging those who are different must be a conscious process. When I started a nonprofit to prevent drowning, building the board of directors was my proudest accomplishment. I intentionally created the perfect "brain." I knew what skills and knowledge were necessary both to run an organization and to address a global epidemic, so I identified the people who most embodied those characteristics. I recruited seven of the smartest and most accomplished people I knew with expertise in risk management, finance, global health, law, epidemiology, medicine, marketing and branding, social marketing, search and rescue, and program development for low-resource environments. Our meetings were fascinating, as we heard very different perspectives on addressing one common goal. The feedback from the board members was consistently positive. Board meetings were a highlight of their professional experience, they genuinely liked and respected each other, and they felt they had learned as much as they contributed.

We had diversity of thought but not by other metrics. We had reasonable gender diversity, six women (including me) and two men, but no diversity in gender identity. Only two countries were represented, with seven Americans and one Brit. There was appallingly little racial diversity, with one Black person and seven white people, especially given the significantly higher drowning rates of Black, Hispanic, and Native American/Indigenous peoples. We were all highly educated, many with multiple degrees or advanced professional designations. We were urban and suburban with no rural experience. And, the most glaring lack of diversity, only one person didn't know me personally before they joined the board because I drew from my spectacularly fabulous but self-selected peer group. Making diversity in experience a priority, even on a small scale, did have an impact, even if we did not represent the true diversity of the eight billion people on Earth. We could all see the benefits.

How you handle diversity makes a difference. Mutual respect and an interest in learning from others made the board a success. A willingness to debate and disagree also stands out in my experience on the steering committee charged with creating the first U.S. National Water Safety Action Plan. The ideas and focus that each person brought to the table were diverse. We all shared the same goal, to create a data-driven plan based on evidence and best practice in drowning prevention, but how that was achieved was not clear cut. Over the three-and-a-half years, there were multiple occasions when we disagreed, sometimes quite starkly. "I disagree" became an opportunity to stop and dig deep into an issue rather than be a divisive moment. I cannot think of a single time when we did not reach an agreement on how to move forward, while still ensuring that everyone felt heard and respected. Groupthink was avoided by establishing a culture of respectful disagreement early in the process.

There is only so much diversity you can achieve in a group. We are all familiar with the corporate photo signifying diversity: one white woman, one Black man, one Hispanic woman, one Asian man. A photo that never represents the actual diversity of an organization but instead reduces people to tokens. No one wants to be a token; it denigrates the true value of what they bring. Unless a clear message is sent that ideas from diverse backgrounds and lived experience are valued, diversity is only lip service. Shifting the intent and execution from tokenism to the representation of diverse interests creates a culture that is more likely to develop solutions to difficult issues.

When creating the U.S. National Water Safety Action Plan, we made a conscious effort to engage professionals across the country who were representative of drowning data. This meant actively pursuing racial diversity and geographic representation. Ninety-six working group members and expert reviewers were involved and over 80 subject matter experts consulted, and 393 individuals from 48 states and 175 organizations at the national, state, county, and local level from 40 states completed the recommendation surveys. We reached out to colleagues from four other countries that had developed national plans. And we still didn't achieve representative diversity. We lagged in engaging high-risk Indigenous populations. There was not proportionally accurate representation of Black, Hispanic, and Asian and rural populations, despite determined outreach. The final plan will not solve drowning, but it is an enormous step forward in capturing the research and expertise of experts from different disciplines across the United States.

Organizations also have a personal preferred communication style. Organizational style falls under the umbrella of corporate culture. IBM has a culture of transformation.[36] Pre-Meta, Facebook's culture was famously "move fast and break things."[37] JP Morgan Chase invites potential hires to "Find your place among a team of talented people who are dedicated to growth, inclusion and innovation."[38] Pepsico's culture statement starts with, "Always do what is right."[39] The culture impacts who they hire and how they conduct business. Sometimes they appear more aspirational than realistic, but they always give a clue to intent and approach.

To identify collaborating organizations, check out their website for their mission, values, or culture statement. You can quickly identify what they value, how they work, and which organizations might be a complementary partner. This applies to for-profits and nonprofits. In the nonprofit world, American Red Cross celebrates, "A culture of belonging: valuing the human in the humanitarian," or human impact orientation.[40] Goodwill Industries asks, "Are you ready to be transformed? … Goodwill provides training, employment and supportive services for people with disabilities or disadvantages who seek greater independence," or long-term community engagement.[41] Amnesty International's first statement is, "We uncover the truth and hold the powerful to account," or action and advocacy.[42] St. Jude's Research Hospital is "leading the way the world understands, treats and defeats childhood cancer and other life-threatening disease," or research.[43]

Coalitions and task forces are successful for a reason; they bring a wide range of communication strategies and programs to address layers of complex issues. Chesterfield Suicide Awareness and Prevention Coalition in Central Virginia brings together a range of organizations working to educate residents about mental illness, risk factors for suicide, and support resources within the community.[44] From county public health departments to FACES, a nonprofit that provides support to families who have a loved one with a brain disorder, they have created a coordinated and united force since 2015, sharing resources and planning events.[45]

Water Safety Task Force Metro Chicago was established in 2018 to create effective policy and set a standard for drowning prevention efforts in the Metro Chicago area.[46] Members include state and city governmental agencies and both large and small nonprofits. As a result, significant collaboration has occurred, programs have been put into place, and, for the first time, an emphasis has been placed on collecting data to inform program and policy development. Key to their success has been integrating a range of styles and approaches. Lurie Children's Hospital has taken the lead in research. Chicago Public Schools strengthened and expanded their aquatics programs, including lifeguard training, which aids the Chicago Park District in addressing the national lifeguard shortage. Both work together in providing awareness and educational programs. Illinois Department of Natural Resources provides significant expertise, funding, support for signage, and deep knowledge about water conditions. The focus of the Chicago Police Department and Chicago Fire Department is primarily on response and rescue, but they also worked with the Park District to incorporate GPS coordinates along the lakefront into the 911 call system and coordinated with the public schools on using school pools off-hours as additional training facilities. Each organization has a different communication style and focus, but by identifying overlapping interests and collaborating, each organization is more effective.

Identify the communication strategies of your competitors to undermine their success. Are they using positive or negative messaging? Are they always on offense or defense? Do they focus on building or destroying community? Are they data-driven or emotionally laden? Do they have strong systems or are they more fly by the seat of their pants? Are your competitors willing to sit at the table and negotiate? Do they come with a list of demands or a willingness to compromise? Do they want to work together or are you at war? Compromise and negotiation require one strategy, that of finding mutual ground and agreeing on the end goal, while war requires another approach.

The idea of war makes many people feel uncomfortable, but history shows humans to be extraordinarily warlike. The evidence of war goes back 5,000 years. There have been over 250 wars in the 20th and 21st centuries alone, not to mention 110 armed conflicts occurring as I write.[47] Like it or not, if your competition to change is thinking in military terms, understanding and strategizing accordingly is necessary. I am never in favor of violence – nonviolent action has a long and successful track record of creating change – but listen when the words being used indicate a martial approach. Showing up with a basket of cupcakes instead of a disarmament strategy is a losing proposition.[48]

The idea of standing together and mutual support is one that most of us recognize and believe in. "All for one, one for all" is a familiar and beloved sentiment from the fictional Three Musketeers.[49] A lofty sentiment, but reality is closer to Benjamin Franklin's more pragmatic take on collaboration: "We must indeed all hang together, or, most assuredly, we shall all hang separately."[50]

Activism is never complete, it is a continuous process, but when you focus on utilizing your unique skills effectively and actively seeking out partners and collaborators with different skills, the process becomes smoother and faster. Convincing people who think differently, who have different skills and a different approach, can be a challenge, as we see in Chapter 3.

Chapter 2 Worksheet

1. What are your top 10 skills? Pull a skills list off the internet or do an online skills assessment.
2. What is your number 1 skill based on what you most enjoy, the skill where you feel you are totally in your zone? Don't judge, don't think of what others want you to do; what does your gut tell you is your number 1 skill? Your "I could do this all day" skill?
3. What skills appear on your aptitude tests?
4. What do others perceive to be your top skills?
5. What three skills do you lack most? Where are you weakest? If you are an organization doing this exercise, what are the top skills of the organization?
6. Are the skills you lack critical to reaching your goals? If so, what people or organizations have the skills that you lack most?
7. Look at your organization, team, or co-activists. How much diversity do you have? Where do you need to expand representation?

Chapter 3

CONVINCING OTHERS TO CARE

We are afraid to care too much, for fear that the other
person does not care at all.

Eleanor Roosevelt[51]

No one cares about your cause. Harsh, offensive, and not strictly true. You care, and you know other people who care. You are connected through organizations, social media, friendship, and work. You have data. Hashtags, protests, statements by influencers, and opinion polls indicate support. There is a lot of noise but the change isn't happening. Not enough people care enough to change their attitudes and behaviors. Worse, the competition is continually adapting, making real change feel elusive, and even reversing change. We have all seen it. History shows a constant tug-of-war.

For an activist, seeing others not care is incredibly frustrating. It feels like a slap in the face. We have all felt the frustration of having a conversation and not connecting. The feeling of "they just don't understand." When your messages aren't getting across, it is easy to blame the audience, not the message. "They don't care about their children." "They are selfish." "They are stupid." "This is important, they should care." A solid indicator that you are at the end of your tether is when you start referring to your target audience as "they." They is an other, someone who does not share the same values or beliefs, someone who is an enemy of change rather than a potential partner in change.

Change your approach. Change how *you* engage with your target audience because people act when we convince them that it is desirable and imperative to act. To change behavior, make the issue relevant to your audience. Be very specific about who you are, what you do, what audience you are trying to reach, and the benefit of changing behavior. Know and understand your competition. It isn't about doing just anything but doing the right things, in the right places, with the right resources. In this chapter, we will look at how to break down your issue, identify your target audience, clarify your role, and identify your competition.

In Chapter 1, the five whys identified the issues you need to address for change to occur, exposed your biases, identified roadblocks, and began to create a roadmap for change. The next step is to identify your target audience. To be clear on your target audience, we ask the five W's: Who? What? Why? Where? and When?

1. *Who* is affected? Whose behavior needs to change? Who can influence the behavior of others? Who is your target audience?

2. *What* behavior change is needed?
3. *Why* will the behavior change help the situation?
4. *Where* is your target audience? In which situations and locations does behavioral change need to occur?
5. *When* should you market the behavior change? Do you need to raise awareness or address other behaviors first?

What resources do you need in place before you can market the behavior change? Is your audience in one location or do you need to reach them in different ways and in different areas?

For every question, link back to the data and research you have and cross-check that you have facts to back up your beliefs. There may not always be data or research for new or innovative ideas, so build in ways of measuring your approach.

Once you have broken down the issue and identified your target audience, clarify your role by taking a hard look at your organization, your areas of expertise, the resources you have available, the target audience you want to reach, and the geographic area you are targeting. Apply your strengths and your weaknesses based on feedback and your personality type. Apply the five whys and W's specifically to your organization to further clarify your role. The goal is to be the best in your particular area of expertise and influence to change behavior.

Communicate your role through your mission statement. A mission statement tells the world "this is who we are," and it sets the true north on your organization's compass. Don't settle for a laundry list of what you offer: "Our mission is to blah, blah, blah." Take the time to make sure your mission is your rallying cry. A mission statement should be specific, inspiring, and include at least three vibrant action verbs, and you should review it annually.

Every organization has a mission statement, but not every organization has an effective mission statement. Look through the websites of organizations you respect and consider successful. Read their mission statements. Pull out those you believe are clear, inspiring, and accurately reflect the organization. Identify why they inspire and use these examples as your inspiration in crafting your mission statement.

The American Red Cross makes good use of action verbs: the organization "prevents and alleviates human suffering in the face of emergencies by mobilizing the power of volunteers and the generosity of donors."[52] The Museum of Modern Art "connects people from around the world to the art of our time."[53] The Peace Corps are clear on their goals: "To promote world peace and friendship through community-based development and intercultural understanding."[54]

You don't need to measure your budget in millions to benefit from a strong mission statement. The International Surf Lifesaving Association (ISLA) took the idea of nailing their colors to the mast to heart and created a longer but very evocative mission statement. ISLA took the time to break down the issue, identify their target audience, and clarify their role. When you read their complete mission statement, there is no mistaking who they are. It ends: "We are water people. We are lifeguards. We are globetrotters. We are activists. We are ISLA."[55] Even if you had never heard of ISLA before, you now have a good idea of what they stand for. ISLA created an internal rallying cry that differentiated them from other organizations, motivated everyone involved with ISLA, and made it easier to engage their target audience and attract funding from like-minded individuals and organizations.

An organization will look different in its start-up phase, middle years, and mature years, and so should your mission statement. A good mission statement keeps the organization focused as good ideas percolate and opportunities arise. Wondering whether you should form a strategic alliance, expand geographically, invest in research, introduce a product, or develop educational materials? Check your mission statement and see if these decisions are aligned with who you are, whether you have outgrown your initial mission statement and need to reclarify your role, or to pass on an opportunity.

The next step is to identify the competition for the behavior change. You cannot effectively influence your target audience if you don't understand the competition for the desired change in attitude and behavior. Competition can take the form of incorrect assessments of risk, lack of knowledge, lack of support, beliefs that are supported by culture, and external factors that support and encourage the behavior. Once you have identified the competition, look at organizations, companies, and cultural norms that support and encourage it. Be aware that these organizations and companies are generally well-funded, well-organized, and excel at marketing effectively. They use marketing to create or support a demand for the current attitudes and behaviors, and simultaneously supply the information, training, products, and experiences to support the damaging behavior.

Unfortunately, negative press and public experience with ineffective or under-marketed programs have resulted in the perception that nonprofits, government agencies, and social change activists throw money away with no measurable results. It is exactly that mentality which has led to belief systems that business can solve big social problems better than government (53% of those surveyed), despite other surveys which show that 59% of Americans want government more involved in solving social problems.[56]

The business solution perception persists, in part, because the positive impact of effective programs has not been marketed effectively to the public. Success has gone unnoticed. Think about it: 97.47% of Americans have access to clean water compared to 73% of people in the world.[57] Do you even think about the clean water in your tap? Can you identify which government entities are responsible for ensuring that clean, uncontaminated water flows from your tap? Chances are you do recognize and purchase bottled water brands, a $98.5 billion market in the United States,[58] or your perception of the level of dangerous tap water is skewed by high-profile stories like the Flint, Michigan crisis.[59] The perception of the magnitude and severity of the problem is distorted. Who is marketing effectively? Not the government, which deserves credit, but the corporations who benefit by selling bottled water. Effective government has been poorly marketed.

The United States Lifesaving Association states that your chance of drowning while swimming at a guarded beach is reduced to 1 in 18 million. In 2023, over 292 million people went to the beach, 87% of the population. Lifeguards rescued 64,578 people and engaged in 9.3 million preventive actions.[60] Did you know that? Probably not, but I am fairly certain you know that Elon Musk bought Twitter, even though only 23% of Americans were active users at the time, a small fraction of the number of people who go to the beach.[61] For-profit activities are 94.4% of gross domestic product (GDP), while nonprofit is 5.6%, yet nonprofits employ 12.3 million people, pay $826 billion in salaries, and purchase over $1 trillion in goods and services, spurring economic activity.[62] The idea that for-profit solutions are the only answer becomes more entrenched, especially in countries like the United States, where capitalism reigns. Capitalism has been effectively marketed.

Breaking down nonprofit budgets further demonstrates who is most effective at marketing their cause. Overall, 49% of nonprofit revenue is fee-for-service.[63] Fee-for-service means that a nonprofit charges for services or programs. The fee-for-service sector is heavily skewed towards hospitals and universities providing medical and education services. Hospitals and universities also comprise many of the 8% of nonprofits which exceed $1 million in size. Hospitals spend modestly on advertising, only $6.2 million in 2023.[64] They have a relatively captive audience, with most patients going to a local hospital, which requires less marketing. Universities in the United States had endowments of $691 billion at the end of 2020, although 33% of that amount is held by just 10 universities.[65] Universities, especially those with high endowments and extremely low acceptance rates, do an exceptional job of marketing the value of their institutions and building brand loyalty among alumni, creating a reliable donor pipeline and a deeply ingrained perception of value in the marketplace, regardless of whether the quality of education is actually superior. Effective marketing at work.

Healthcare in the United States was 17.3% of GDP in 2022, a healthy 4.1% increase in one year.[66] This compares to 9.83% of GDP globally and 12.49% for high-income countries. Healthcare in the United States is profitable, even for nonprofits, but the profits do not reflect quality of care. A recent study showed that the United States ranked ninth or tenth of 10 peer countries. Americans pay a premium for the lowest health outcomes and access to care, and come ninth for administrative efficiency and equity.[67] Healthcare delivered as fee-for-service directly impacts patients. About a third of the 100 million adults in the United States with healthcare debt owe money for hospitalization. Half owe at least $5,000. A quarter owe $10,000 or more.[68] Nonprofit hospitals must provide charity care as a condition of their tax-exempt status, but the net operating margin for hospital and healthcare facilities in January 2024 was still 5.12%. For context, financial services (non-bank and insurance) enjoy a net operating margin of 15.44% and oil and gas production and exploration 28.26%. This compares to 8.54% for the total market and 33.41% for the total market without financials.[69]

Meanwhile, 72% of nonprofit hospitals don't follow through on community investment commitments, leaving $17 billion uninvested.[70] The World Health Organization assesses that 72% of Americans rate their healthcare quality positively, despite ranking 37th out of 191 countries, below a number of high-income countries.[71] The United States ranks low on dimensions of access, efficiency, and equity. Maternal mortality rates are 5.6 per 1,000 live births, more than three times the rate for most other high-income countries and higher than most Organisation for Economic Co-operation and Development (OECD) countries. Interestingly, between the time I wrote this section and did the final fact check, United States data had been removed from the OECD site.[72]

Omission tells a story. The United States ranks first only for cost, not outcomes. Effective marketing at work.

It is beyond my comprehension that any sane country depends on a sick and weakened population to fuel economic growth. It seems to be a huge economic and security risk for 18.3% of GDP to be dependent on increasing and sustainable sickness, but the successful marketing of the healthcare system and treating illness far exceeds the marketing budget for preventing illness. Spending on preventive care has declined from an already paltry 3.7% in 2000 to 2.9% in 2018.[73] Treatment is marketed far more aggressively than prevention.

Carving out the 49% of fee-for-service, which is skewed to healthcare and universities, 31.8% of nonprofit revenue comes from government grants and contracts. Priorities are determined by data, political ideologies, and lobbyists. Philanthropists make large donations, playing an outsize role in both prioritizing and solving global problems. Some 8.9% of registered 501(c)(3) organizations are private foundations. This includes some of the largest reservoirs of cash, with the top 50 private foundations holding $229.6 billion, not including the Chan Zuckerberg Initiative, which is organized as a limited liability corporation and funded with Meta stock.[74] Effective marketing of financial priorities has promoted significant tax benefits and social status for major donors.

The bottom line is that 88% of nonprofit budgets are operating on a shoestring budget of under $500,000 annually, which doesn't get you very far these days. Exhibit A is the drowning prevention field. In the United States, drowning is the leading cause of death among children aged 1–4 and the second leading cause of unintentional injury death in children aged 0–17, but drowning prevention and water safety don't even make the National Institutes of Health list for funding.[75] Following dedicated diplomacy and effective presentation of the issue and solutions (marketing) from a dedicated group of people, Bloomberg Philanthropies generously funded the development of both World Health Organization reports on drowning and a long-term study on effective survival swim techniques in Southeast Asia.[76] With their financial support, drowning prevention efforts have moved swiftly forward in the last 10 years. In May 2024, Bloomberg Philanthropies announced another $60 million of funding for programs in Bangladesh, Ghana, India, Uganda, Vietnam, and 10 states in the United States with high numbers of drowning deaths.[77] Their $104 million total commitment has impacted the global drowning prevention community far beyond the programs they have directly funded. Without the initial marketing of the issue by a few individuals and organizations, change would have continued to be fragmented and limited. Money makes a material difference.

Changes in attitude and behavior have the greatest impact, requiring the slow and unglamorous slog of awareness, education, and skills-based training. Long-term solutions, like swimming lessons, learning to rescue others safely, pool fencing, and life jackets cost relatively little, but the benefits have not been quantified financially. Little work has been done on marketing the benefits of learning to swim, including higher cognition and better performance in school, to create a demand for water safety education and skills-based training.[78] Even less has been done on explaining the substantial costs and emotional trauma not incurred by preventing drowning. The total estimated cost of fatal drowning in the United States in 2022 was $48.87 million in medical costs and $60.23 billion in "value of statistical life," meaning the benefit of avoiding a fatality or what a life contributes to society if it is not cut short.[79] The numbers don't include the costs of nonfatal drowning. For every child that dies from drowning, another seven or eight are taken to the emergency room and 40% are admitted for further care, but medical coding lacks the consistency to capture these costs accurately.[80] Cohesive strategies and campaigns take time and money.

Despite the barriers, progress has been made. Globally, Australia led the way, creating their first national plan in 1998.[81] Canada, the UK, and New Zealand followed their lead, all with central government support.[82] In 2014, WaterSafety USA was formed.[83] WaterSafety USA is a consortium of leading governmental and nonprofits in the drowning prevention field, but unlike most countries, it does not have cabinet-level representation. Following a 2017 recommendation by the World Health Organization for each country to create a national water safety plan, WaterSafety USA committed to creating the first U.S. Water Safety Action Plan, published in May 2023.[84] The field is long on passion and creativity but short on cash and people.

Almost everything is easier with enough money and support, but an enormous amount can be accomplished with neither. Remember that every tactic discussed in this chapter is already being used effectively in support of negative attitudes and behaviors that are rarely supported by the majority. The tactics outlined here may not be visible to the average person, but successful enterprises, both legal and illegal, understand this. Know what is being done to you. Understand that there is no reason why you cannot apply the same principles to promoting and supporting positive behavioral changes that benefit both individuals and society.

Roe v. Wade upheld reproductive rights for 50 years, until it was reversed in 2022. The Stonewall uprising that ignited the LGBTQ+ movement took place in 1969, but it took 47 years before gay marriage became legal. The arc from women's suffrage to the 19th Amendment giving women the right to vote was around 70 years. Voting rights for African Americans took the 14th, 15th, and 24th Amendment, plus the Voting Rights Act, a staggering 97 years, and rights are still being undermined. Climate change as a result of the greenhouse effect was first identified in 1896. The impact of fossil fuels has been studied by ExxonMobil since the 1970s, but effective marketing by the fossil fuel industry to downplay and divert attention meant that the first United Nations climate conference didn't occur until 1990, and aggressive resistance to change by industry and some governments has left us drastically off target for offsetting the impact of a warming planet.[85]

Most social issues are currently polarized. In my small community, even a school funding referendum and the election of the village president became deeply polarizing contentious events in recent years. Remember the SARS pandemic? Zika? Ebola?[86] They likely did not disrupt your daily life because the response was based on healthcare protocols and science, not politics. The COVID-19 death toll was far higher in counties in the United States where it became a polarizing political issue.[87] The pendulum of time will surely swing back to a period of compromise and mutual respect on a national and global level, but in this time of absolutism, continuing negotiations when the competition sees only a zero-sum game is both foolish and destructive. If your competition is operating on a war footing, adopt wartime strategies focusing on weakening or eliminating the competition. Divide and conquer. Divide by encouraging turf wars within the competition. Sow seeds of doubt and mistrust among their existing partners. Simultaneously identify and engage individuals or organizations that may be open to discussion. Identify common ground. Support their work to create a potential partner without creating a new competitor. Cull doubters from the herd. Identify influencers, power players, and ordinary people who are uncomfortable or disgusted with the status quo. Offer them an alternative way forward, but in their words and their communication style, not yours. Whenever possible, move towards collaboration and a win-win outcome, away from zero-sum, but don't be afraid to fight fire with fire when warranted.

The true measure of caring enough is a measurable change in attitudes and behaviors. It isn't sharing a post or wearing a bracelet, it is showing up at a school board meeting, running for office, or committing to writing letters to elected officials. Change is measured in donations, attendance at events, swimming class registrations filling up, car seats fitted correctly, the number of solar panels installed, and voter turnout. Measuring change is the only true measure of whether your strategy is working.

Chapter 3 Worksheet

The issue: Five Whys?

1. Why?
2. Why?
3. Why?
4. Why?
5. Why?

The issue: Five W's

1. Who?
2. What?
3. Why?
4. Where?
5. When?

Clarify your role

- Diversity of team:
- Areas of expertise:
- Resources available:
- Target audience:
- Geographic area:
- Strengths:
- Weaknesses:

The organization: Five Whys

1. Why?
2. Why?
3. Why?

4. Why?
5. Why?

The organization: Five W's

1. Who?
2. What?
3. Why?
4. Where?
5. When?

Develop your mission statement

- Bigger issue:
- Issue we will address:
- Target audience:
- Action verbs:
    1.
    2.
    3.
- Mission statement:

Chapter 4

DATA IS
THE KEY

Data, data, data! … I can't make bricks without clay!

Arthur Conan Doyle[88]

Data is a hot topic. Type the word "data" into Google and you come up with over 18 billion results, also known as metadata, or data on data. Six years ago, the same search yielded six billion results, demonstrating that our obsession with data is rapidly accelerating. On the surface, data is a fairly dry subject, defined as "factual information (such as measurements or statistics) used as a basis for reasoning, discussion, or calculation"[89] – typically not a subject to cause widespread excitement.

Humans create structures to make sense of their environment. As the world becomes more populated and more complex, data has gained in importance. Data is a useful tool for breaking down complexity into more manageable pieces. We need data to identify problems, create and measure programs, and identify contributing factors. Increasingly, those who fund social change initiatives require data-driven programs. This may be because a number of the individuals and organizations currently holding the purse strings possess their wealth because of their own use of, and bias towards, data-driven solutions. Of the 25 most philanthropic billionaires in 2022, 18 gained their wealth through the finance and tech industries.[90] Michael Bloomberg stated, "You can't manage what you don't measure." And "In God we trust. Everyone else: bring data."[91]

More than at any time in our history, data is recognized as an important tool to help us simplify the complexity of our world, and we have an unprecedented ability to capture and manipulate huge amounts of it. However, the role of data in resolving social issues is not straightforward.

Data is always imperfect. Structures for gathering and reporting data may be flawed or missing. To make sense of data, we need human interpretation, with its inherent individual, cultural, geographic, and societal biases. Give one set of raw data to two analysts at opposite ends of the political spectrum, and you will end up with two opposite but compelling arguments for change. As the economist Ronald Coase said, "If you torture the data long enough, nature will always confess."[92]

In this chapter, we will discuss why you need data to put your cause on the agenda, the weaknesses in data, what to do when data is insufficient or not available, and what to do with data. We also look at how the current focus on data is causing inadvertent discrimination against the causes and groups most in need of funding and recognition.

The importance of data to put your cause on the agenda cannot be understated. Without data, it is challenging to convince anyone that there is a problem or to attract funding. Without data, you don't know where to target your efforts or how to measure your efforts. You don't know if you are solving the problem, creating new problems, or if the proposed solution has unintended consequences that make the cure worse than the disease.

Many causes rely on emotion to engage supporters and attract funding. This continues to be a successful approach because people respond far more to emotion than they do numbers and facts, despite the current obsession with data.[93] A study showed that individuals who experience more intense feelings achieved higher decision-making performance.[94] As much as we wish to believe in the rationality of humans, even economists are starting to understand that humans do not act rationally and often act in a way that is counter to their own well-being and the optimal outcome.[95] Irrationality explains the popularity of lotteries, the fear of air travel when traffic accidents are a bigger killer, and why people regard terrorism as a major concern while overlooking the significantly higher probability that their children will be killed by a gun in their own home.[96] Emotion regularly tops logic in decision-making.

While emotion is an effective way to engage your audience to change their attitudes and behaviors, data is necessary to separate "it works" from "it feels right" approaches. There is fatigue and frustration over a seeming lack of progress on many issues, despite the huge amount of time and money that have been thrown at those issues. This is likely because emotion and data are not being leveraged together to achieve optimal results.

Raw data is unemotional, clean, and unbiased, but data without context and interpretation is also useless. Take the number one. *One* on its own means nothing. If I add the context of *"one person drowned,"* you might think it is a shame. When I say, *"one person drowns every 80 seconds,"* it is a bit shocking but still removed. If I say, *"one of my neighbors drowned yesterday,"* it suddenly makes drowning much more real, something that happens to people you know, something that could happen to you.

Data doesn't just happen. Data is influenced by those who request data, those who pay for data, and those who gather data. These decisions are in turn influenced by personal bias; cultural and societal norms regarding gender, race, and religion; lobbyists;

outside interests; finances; and the physical ability to capture data. Increasingly, the accumulation, manipulation, and utilization of data is influenced by a very small group of people whose ideology poses a direct threat to activists, specifically a subset of those funding and promoting the expansion of AI. Even that bastion of conservative free market capitalism, the *Financial Times*, raised the alarm over a subset of backers, libertarians like Elon Musk and Peter Thiel who are behind the funding of AI, stating that, "Washington needs to put a titanium fence around AI."[97]

More broadly, libertarians are a direct threat to all activism designed to benefit most of society and the world as a whole. They interpret author Ayn Rand's message that selfishness, strictly defined as "concern with one's own interests," is separate from moral evaluation and that humans are designed to be pitted against one another, despite considerable evidence to the contrary.[98] Libertarians have exploited financial and legal structures to amass extraordinary levels of wealth and bend systems to their will. As Peter Thiel memorably stated in his Cato Institute essay, "Since 1920, the vast increase in welfare beneficiaries and the extension of the franchise to women – two constituencies that are notoriously tough for libertarians – have rendered the notion of 'capitalist democracy' into an oxymoron." He goes on to say that the internet (along with the ocean and space) are the vehicles to "impact and force change on the existing social and political order."[99] Make no mistake, many of the (mostly) billionaire men pushing AI are implementing their own world view, one which adversely affects most of the other people on the planet. They are direct competition to much social change.

Putting aside the personal belief systems of some of those pushing AI, it is also inherently biased. Bias is introduced by those who program AI, those who fund AI projects, those who head up companies creating and disseminating AI, and the data being scraped. The bias towards a male perspective is overwhelming and concerning: 80% of AI professors are male,[100] and 85% of AI researchers at Facebook and 90% at Google are male. Racial diversity is even worse, with 88% of AI industry decision-makers being privileged white Anglo males, according to AI Now Institute's 2019 study.[101] Women and minorities are underrepresented in published research papers, senior executive positions, clinical trials, and more, further skewing the data being scraped. Concerns about the inherent bias in AI impacting healthcare are already being raised by organizations including the National Institutes of Health (inherent biases and disparities) and the National Education Association (negative affect on non-native English speakers).[102] An article in the *Harvard Business Review* addressed the broad business implications from "baking in and deploying biases at scale" on everything from hiring to criminal justice risk assessments to exhibiting and reinforcing gender stereotyping.[103] Controlling who collects data and what data is collected already ensures that any analysis of the data is inaccurate, given that the data is not representative of the global population.

The bias is exacerbated by lack of context. Context gives data importance. Data can tell us that infant mortality is spiking in an area, but it takes experts who interpret the data to make sense of the context, the all-important why. Anthropologists, historians, sociologists, social scientists, aid workers, geologists, doctors, lawyers, biologists; all these areas of expertise and more are needed to assess the data and put it into a fuller context. When priorities, analysis, and interpretation are set by a fairly homogeneous group, it is impossible to see the full story. Societal inequalities can be easily masked or overlooked by the way we collect and categorize data. Researchers follow established protocols designed to eliminate personal bias, but even deciding what to study is subject to personal bias.

You undoubtedly know what data exists for your issue. It is equally important to identify the data that does not exist, the inherent biases, and where the data does not tell the entire story. Pointing to the lack of data or demonstrating how data masks an issue creates the full story. Take death. Death seems straightforward. A simple piece of data. However, in many countries, drowning isn't counted as a cause of death, which means that, according to the data, drowning is not an issue that needs to be addressed. Drowning data is not available for 59% of World Health Organization member countries, including most of Africa and Asia. There are several reasons why drowning is not counted as a cause of death in these countries. Many countries don't have the ability to capture deaths that occur outside of a hospital, and most drowning deaths occur quickly and far away from a hospital. Some cultures hold entrenched beliefs in river gods or fate as the cause of death. Fear of prosecution by the authorities for murder or neglect can lead to underreporting. In this case, the lack of data tells as much of a story as having data – but only if we insist on telling the full story.

Always follow the money. Money is an important data point. Someone always pays to collect and analyze data. In an ideal data world, resources are always fairly distributed with no inherent bias. We live in the real world where, despite global attempts to capture data cleanly and equitably, gathering data and the interpretation of that data is subject to economic interests. Every country has their share of graft, corruption, lobbying, and attempts to influence policy and spending. Like it or not, there is always more than one way to slice and dice the data to tell a story. There will always be circumstances where the money paying for the report or the person preparing the report will insert a bias. These groups or industries are formidable competition.

Bias can work to your advantage. Follow the money and you will learn much about your competition. Get on their email and calling distribution lists. Follow them on social media. Data on finances, also known as budgets, often tells a clear story, especially if you follow the trail to the original sources. Look closely at the budgets of your competition. Follow the sources of funding. Look past the rhetoric to the numbers, both the big numbers and the line-item numbers.

The big numbers include money spent on marketing and lobbying. If you are working on any issue impacted by the climate crisis, you are up against the largest industry in the world by revenue, oil and gas exploration and production.[104] If you are working on an issue that uses behavior change to improve health and wellness, you are up against the biggest spender of lobbying dollars in the United States, the pharmaceutical and health products industry.[105] Billions of dollars in revenue and lobbying buys a lot of marketing expertise, influence, and data.

Line-item numbers refer to specific parts of a budget. And budgets reflect bias. In past years, the Internal Revenue Service budget was steadily and strategically cut to protect wealthy individuals and corporations while increasing the pressure on low-income taxpayers, facilitating the transfer of wealth to the top.[106] To weaken environmental oversight at the Environmental Protection Agency, rather than slashing cuts, Congress quietly cut the line-item travel and investigator budgets, forcing regulators and scientists to rely on self-reporting by the industries they oversee.[107] This is as effective as calling your teenager when you are out of town and asking if they are having any parties. Just because the beer cans were removed from the premises doesn't mean the party didn't happen.

Aldous Huxley said, "Facts do not cease to exist because they are ignored," [108] but a lack of data makes it harder to convince people of the need to focus on an issue or change behavior. If you are working in a field where there is limited data, where the data doesn't tell the whole story, or where your competition is skewing the presentation of data, tell the story of the existing data and the lack of data.

Develop an economic argument for change using indirect data. In other words, if you can't get in the front door, go around to the back, climb in a window, or tunnel under the foundations. For this argument, you need to enlist economists, finance experts, and researchers to your cause. We don't have great data on drowning, but we do have enough information to begin building a solid economic case for promoting and teaching water safety. We know that teaching water skills creates economic opportunities by opening up a range of professions. We know that nonfatal drowning injuries in countries like the United States often result in significant medical expenses, including permanent brain damage, which places a significant financial burden on medical systems, insurance companies, and families. We know that when an economically productive adult dies, this has a measurable negative impact on the well-being of their children, in addition to being an economic loss to a country. Research supports the argument that early childhood programs "pay for themselves."[109] We know that children often drown after significant investments have been made in vaccinations and education. In the United States, four-sided pool fencing, life jackets, swim lessons, supervision, and lifeguards are all proven to reduce drowning deaths and injuries.[110] In a study in Bangladesh, the combination of a creche (day care) and SwimSafe swimming lessons was found to be very cost-effective.[111] Drowning prevention programs are a solid investment.

Maximize the effectiveness of solid data by putting it into a financial context. Spell out the cost–benefit analysis which shows that the proposed behavioral change benefits your target population. Compare the cost of your proposed behavioral change to the existing reality. Work with your strategic partners to bring in a wider range of data to tell a more complete story and to demonstrate that combining resources provides a greater return on investment. Child drowning alone was estimated to cost $16.92 billion in 2020.[112] The average lifetime medical and work loss-related cost per hospitalization for drowning was estimated to be $292,300 in 2010.[113] By contrast, a creche incorporating early childcare education, plus teaching hand washing, provides a bigger return on investment than individual interventions, reducing drowning deaths by 83%, plus the reduction in illness and death from diarrhea.[114] It is not an apples-to-apples comparison because the case study was in Bangladesh and the medical costs were in the United States, but it is the only data we have right now. To provide context, nonfatal drownings generally don't happen in low-resource environments because of access to medical care. In low-resource environments, there are mostly fatal drownings.

Don't fall into the trap of gathering data just for the sake of it, but do collect data. There is good data and bad data. Whether you are a small organization with a few faithful volunteers or a large organization with a decent budget and staff, find out what the baseline measurements are in your field of interest and make sure that the data you are collecting is captured and measured in a way that would be considered best practice. Use the network of strategic alliances you have created to spread the word about what data should be collected. Share the data. Don't limit yourself to the data you think is important, and collect the data that major funding organizations are requesting. Data can tell a powerful story, but only if it is consistent and collected from a wide range of sources.

Once you have the data, use it. Liberate the numbers from their spreadsheets and integrate them into your work. Data will help you increase the effectiveness of your programs. It will help you tailor strategies and interventions for maximum impact and minimum cost and effort. Learn what works, who you need to reach, and what techniques actually change behavior. Promote the proof of your success in the form of data. Lead people down the path you want them to follow, balancing the emotion and the data to create a compelling story.

One inherent weakness in the current focus on data-driven solutions is the inadvertent discrimination against those causes and groups that most need funding and recognition. Some of the world's most intransigent problems involve people with the fewest resources or lack of relevant education, which limits their ability to promote or resolve their issues with data. Tying data to funding perpetuates the historic tendency of sending in outside aid groups to solve local problems when local groups have little or no hope of meeting the data criteria for funding. The current focus on data is a positive step forward, but it is not the final answer to solving the world's problems. In our push to spend money wisely and effectively, we have created another hurdle that will force some groups to become dependent on outside help, if only to gather and analyze data, without offering the tools to limit or ultimately eliminate this dependence. We have created a model for change that favors those with wealth and power, which allows them to set the agenda based on their personal biases.

Data-driven solutions can hinder creativity in solving difficult problems. Sometimes, solutions or problems defy data because the ideas are so unique and innovative that the ramifications of the proposed solutions are far outside the comprehension of most people. "How do we measure?" must be developed after the fact or on the go. Data can stifle the visionaries who challenge the status quo and suggest we are measuring the wrong things. Leonardo da Vinci and Galileo wouldn't get funding today because there would be no data to justify their inventions. The reliance on data can blind us to common sense. Common sense tells us that not knowing how to swim means the chance of drowning if you fall into water unexpectedly is high. The current data requirements require that to be proven.

Several things need to happen to balance the inadvertent inequality that has resulted from the current focus on data-driven solutions. The first is that a mechanism needs to be created that trains organizations around the world about data, regardless of size or funding. The second is that we need to rethink how we collect data.

Capturing and reporting data does not have to be complex. Numbers are simple. The UK and Australia have developed independent databases to track drowning in their countries using news reports.[115] Tracking drowning using Google and newspaper reports has also been instrumental in establishing drowning rates in Nepal and Uganda, where there has been little or no official drowning data.[116]

Teach potential grant recipients how to collect data, how to use data, and how to report data. Bring along everyone to a basic level of data fluency. This can be accomplished through simple online courses with criteria agreed upon by government agencies and major grantors. Include students and faculty in the social sciences to translate tech ideas into language and concepts that can be easily understood and interpreted correctly and that are accepted culturally. We don't need to create experts in data, we just need to create a basic fluency that will enable all organizations to measure results and use those results to improve their programs and be financially viable. Once basic fluency exists, we can use that fluency to fill the gaps in the official data. We know there are large gaps in the official data, despite concerted efforts to collect and standardize data. We cannot measure what is not reported. There must be a broader understanding of what should be reported, and how.

It is idealistic to assume that the tech industries would fund such an initiative, but if a financial argument were made that transitioning a sector of the economy towards better and more informed users of tech products, perhaps that would provide a nudge. At this point in time, the tech industry is both a potential collaborator and a primary competitor. Given the importance of data and the relative youth of the industry, it is too soon to predict how that tension will play out.

Privacy issues related to gathering data rightly raise serious concerns. If we move towards enlisting more organizations and the public to help us gather data, the concerns will be magnified. There is enormous potential for the misuse and manipulation of data, as well as the negative repercussions stemming from privacy and security issues. This is an ongoing issue, but it should not be used as an excuse not to explore new ways of collecting and verifying data. After all, data is already being collected and misused by bad actors, so there is enormous room for improvement. We need to create a framework where data is verifiable by third-party sources and sanitized (made free of identifying information). We also need to integrate security, but since security already cannot be guaranteed, it is better to ensure that the data cannot harm an individual when it is hacked.

We can explore new ways of collecting data. The young tech-savvy group ISLA created Global Drowning Tracker to harness technology in a more forward-thinking manner. The technology was put aside when the organization moved in a different direction, but it had the potential to drastically change how data is gathered and disseminated in any number of other fields by creating a conversation between policymakers and those impacted by policies. The public and designated researchers input data, which was cross-checked against news reports or official sources to verify, sanitize, and categorize the data for analysis. Data input could be done via a computer or SMS messaging, which meant that the 90% of the world's eight billion people who had a cell phone also had a voice. When you ask the public to participate in collecting data, you send clear messages that an issue is of importance and that their individual experience is of importance. When you have engaged an individual and made their experience matter, it is more likely that they will become an ambassador for change and be open to the desired behavioral change. It shifts both power and responsibility to individuals, inviting them to set the agenda and develop solutions.

There will likely be unmitigated horror at official levels at the thought of the public self-reporting. There are legitimate concerns regarding the veracity of data, privacy, and possible abuse of the system that need to be addressed, but the powerful potential of creating a pincer movement between official data and public engagement should not be ignored. The beast created by the internet and big data already exists, so we need to learn how to ride the beast, to train the beast to deliver the information we need. For instance, there is no reason why simple algorithms cannot be built into Global Drowning Tracker or similar software to prompt reporting through a series of steps and then funnel that data into appropriate International Classification of Diseases (ICD)-10 codes. It isn't perfect, but if we start to gather data, verify the data, and then break it down as much as possible, we are miles ahead. There is power in reaching out to victims, engaging them, and counting their experience – in slavery, human trafficking, bullying, discrimination, corruption, abuse, and drowning.

Engaging the public to gather data and providing them with the tools to change their behavior will cause a shift in power that will be resisted, but the shift has already begun. It is better to manage the pendulum shift proactively rather than have the pendulum swing wildly. Decisions can no longer be only top-down and enforced. Change from only one direction has a limited chance of lasting success. Use the structure of organizations to make sense of data, to identify and develop methods for creating change, and to communicate the change to the public. Harness both bottom-up and top-down power to identify desired behavioral change, develop solutions, and create and implement programs that are measurable, cost-effective, and sustainable.

Chapter 4 Worksheet

1. What data do you currently have?
2. Where does your data come from?
3. What story does your data tell?
4. What data do you lack?
5. What resources currently exist that could collect the data (e.g., future collaborators)?
6. What story does your lack of data tell?
7. What data do your competitors use?
8. Who in your organization, or in your circle, understands how to manipulate, analyze, and use data?
9. How can you use data more effectively to support behavior change initiatives and engage funders?

REAL CHANGE REQUIRES BEHAVIORAL CHANGE

Data are just summaries of thousands of stories – tell a
few of those stories to help make the data meaningful.

Chip Heath and Dan Heath[117]

Data is reassuringly sterile. Data is simple. It is the translation of data into internalized and sustainable change that is complicated. Internalized change means that people reach a point where they don't need to be reminded of the correct behavior; it is reflexive, just as we automatically fasten our seat belt when we get in a car. Sustainable change means the behavior is passed down through generations, just as we automatically ask our children to buckle up.

Data can tell us what needs to change. Data can measure both expected change and unintended outcomes. But data cannot make people change. Plato believed that human behavior flows from three main sources: desire, emotion, and knowledge. Notice that Plato does not mention numbers, logic, or data. Knowledge may come from the facts that data provides, but knowledge without desire and emotion does not create real change in behavior. To change behavior, you must make the change desirable, even compelling. People must *want* to change.

Too often, we decide that if we just issue dire warnings based on the data, people will listen. After all, how could anyone engage in damaging activities given the comprehensive amount of data arguing against these activities? The problem is that humans may appear to agree with the logical arguments, but they are adept at lying to themselves, their loved ones, and the authority figures in their lives.

"I don't smoke anymore … except when I have a glass of wine."

"I'm exercising regularly and eating right … it's just a few spoonfuls of ice cream straight out of the carton at midnight."

"I always use a condom during sex."

Caveats, exceptions to the rule, and definitive statements that don't match the data. Humans know what behavior is expected, but it doesn't mean they are following through. Contrary to the definitive statement about always using condoms, heterosexual men consistently report higher condom use than women, yet men also report pressuring women to have sex without condoms and in no country is condom use anywhere close to 100%.[118] It is likely that a large segment of the public knows what they should be doing but doesn't want to admit to doing otherwise, backed up by evidence that condom use among adolescents is declining.[119] They have all heard the dire warnings and know the correct behavior, but the data tells us that there is rather large amount of wiggle room behind closed doors.

Sustainable, internalized behavioral change means that people don't lie to themselves. Sustainable change means the new behavior occurs regularly – every time you get in the car, you fasten your seatbelt. Internalized change means the new behavior requires no conscious thought – buckling up is a reflex. The greatest return on investment in positive behavior change occurs when each individual takes ownership of the new behavior and follows through without prompting. Even better if they become an ambassador for the new behavior and teach others. In this chapter, we will discuss the positive means of changing behavior – the carrot.

To change behavior, you need to identify the desired change, communicate the desired change, model the desired change, measure both intended and unintended outcomes, and continually assess whether the desired change is achieving your goal.

1. IDENTIFY THE DESIRED CHANGE

Once you understand the big picture, the five whys and W's, use data to identify the problem and the behaviors that need to change. Identify scenarios that are contributing to the problem and begin to develop possible solutions. Brainstorm a wide range of potential solutions. Single or "obvious" solutions rarely succeed. Look at the full range of behavioral changes that might change the outcome and break them down to see which changes are realistic to implement. Look at the culture, the geography, the cost of implementing the change, and the barriers to change. Begin to expand upon and test reasonable and attainable behavior change.

According to UNICEF, 2-year-olds drown at the highest rate in Bangladesh. Using data, it was determined that children were most likely to drown at certain times of day. Digging deeper, it was found that young children were wandering off and drowning in open water because they were not being properly supervised while their mothers focused on household tasks. Open water is a threat everywhere, but with 75% of Bangladesh underwater, the environment cannot be changed. One approach to behavior change would be to tell mothers to watch their children more carefully between the peak drowning hours of 10am to 2pm, the time when mothers are preparing meals and doing household tasks. Promoting such a behavior change is totally unrealistic. It goes against the societal expectations of women in that culture, and no one can watch a child 100% of the time, especially a boundary-pushing and age-appropriately exploring 2-year-old. Researchers are testing two realistic behavior changes. First, young children attend a creche (preschool), which was shown in earlier studies to reduce drowning in the target population by 82% and also provides additional health and education benefits to children and parents. The second behavior change is to support the production and use of locally produced playpens crafted out of environmentally sustainable and inexpensive bamboo. The playpens contain young children when they are at home and direct supervision is not possible, as well as providing additional benefits to the community through new business opportunities.[120]

Every behavioral change has a ripple effect that needs to be recognized, both expected and unexpected. It was expected (and confirmed with data) that a creche would reduce drowning rates. In a different case, it was expected that insecticide-infused bed nets would be effective in preventing malaria, but it was an unexpected outcome that the nets would instead be used as fishing nets, having no impact on malaria rates and leading to increased pollution of local waters.[121]

At every step in the process, test the changes. Measure the attitudes, behaviors, and outcomes – expected and unexpected.

2. COMMUNICATE THE DESIRED CHANGE

Once you have identified behavior changes that result in the desired outcome, communicate the desired change to your target population. To market the behavior effectively, dissect the behaviors into manageable components; use words understandable at no higher than an 8-year-old's level of vocabulary and grammar using local language; do not use abbreviations, acronyms, or technical terms; and keep it simple, consistent, positive, and repetitive across a range of media.

Make the issue and the behavior change relevant to your audience and then focus on the positive. The answer to the question, "Why should I care?" is often, "So you don't die, get hurt, or suffer," but the volume of warnings and the sheer number of things that can kill or harm you can overload the most diligent and concerned person. Make the behavior change relevant and desirable. In the case of a campaign to change the habit of open defecation by introducing toilets in a low-resource environment, the first attempt of simply building toilets was unsuccessful. The beautifully built structures were instead used as shrines, since they were some of the newest and most robustly built structures in the community. There was no context for the buildings and no communication and marketing campaign. Activists pivoted, and in an effective marketing campaign, asked people to drink a glass of water filled with human waste, which was predictably greeted with disgust. They then explained that it is essentially what happens when you don't use toilets. They explained why people should care, and behaviors changed.[122]

Another technique is to broaden the issue or narrow your audience. Both can be done simultaneously. To address wildlife poaching, broadening the issue by linking individual species to national pride has helped to save the Philippine eagle and the American bald eagle from extinction.[123] Narrowing the audience works by engaging specific populations in the community who will be hurt by the environmental disruption, the loss of tourist dollars, or some other contribution to their sustenance or culture if the animals disappear.

Uniting the public against a common enemy has a long and effective history. Negatively, it manifests as xenophobia, but unifying can be used positively to identify and root out narcissistic actions, organized criminal behavior, or ingrained cultural beliefs that are harmful or benefit only a few. News reports of Saudi princes hunting the endangered Houbara bustard in Pakistan, wealthy Chinese hunting endangered polar bears, and Minnesota dentist Walter Palmer killing Cecil the Lion in Zimbabwe and an endangered Mongolian ram sparked outrage abroad and locally, opening the door to creating positive changes in attitudes towards protecting endangered animals in those countries.[124]

Get to the crux of the problem and explain the situation in a way that has meaning for your audience. When you are deeply embedded in any issue, it is easy to forget that nothing is "obvious" or "common sense." It is even harder to communicate what you know is a complex and nuanced range of behaviors in no more than three simple steps – the most that most people can reliably remember.

Step outside of your own deep knowledge bank and think of someone who doesn't know what you are talking about. Your parents. Your grandparents. Your children. Your best friend in a totally different field. Create your own private test audience. What is the one most important thing they need to know? What three steps should they take? How will you explain it so they understand? Don't assume – try your message on a real person. My mom was an elementary school teacher, very creative and people oriented. My dad was an engineer, precise and data oriented. Individually, and together, they made a great test audience (and parents). Both were smart, but neither had knowledge of drowning prevention, so if I was getting blank looks or not receiving the response I had expected, I knew I needed to refine my message.

After you have broken down the most desired behaviors into no more than three instructions, communicate them in simple, unambiguous, and nontechnical language. If someone from your test audience cannot understand, follow instructions accurately, and remember the instructions three months later, your campaign is unlikely to succeed. You don't want to wow people with your years of experience or boggle their mind with the depth of your knowledge; you want to change their behavior.

When my children were very young, we had a pool. I set the rule that they could not go down the steps to the fenced pool without me. After the inevitable and unending queries of "why?" I finally got down to brass tacks: "If I'm not with you, and you fall in the water, you might not see me again." I laid out the consequences in language they would understand. I did not need to wow them with my knowledge of the drowning process, human physiology, academic studies on the issue, existential musings on death, or my fluency in big and important words. All that was irrelevant and unimaginable to my audience. "You won't see mom again" is real and relevant to a young child. "Don't go near the pool without mom" is clear, unambiguous, and directive language. I balanced the message with regular hours of fun pool time to positively reinforce the message that swimming *with* mom was a desirable and rewarding behavior.

3. MODEL THE DESIRED CHANGE

Provide both the action and consequence in simple, directive, and unambiguous language, consistently and repetitively, until the action is internalized. If (action), then (consequence). "If you touch the fire, then you will get burned." "If you drink and drive, then you might kill yourself or someone else." "If you cross the street without looking both ways, then you might get hit by a car and killed." Often, we simply give the desired behavior without explaining the consequences, which reduces the chance that the behavior will be remembered or even understood correctly. A study showed that simply telling young children to "look both ways before you cross the street" resulted in no understanding of why. One memorable response to the researcher's question of "Why do you look both ways?" was "to look for superheroes?"[125] No one had explained the consequences.

Know your audience. "You will never see me again" worked with my audience. My children wouldn't take my instructions as a desirable challenge, unlike a friend's child, who would have immediately tested the limits by scaling the fence. How you communicate and change behavior will require a range of strategies to interact effectively with different audiences. The techniques and methods of communication used to convince a teenage boy to change his behavior are different from those you would use to reach mothers, the elderly, or the very young – never mind cultural or geographic challenges. In a video promoting responsible drinking, Budweiser targeted a relationship that would pull at the heartstrings of many a young man.[126] They showed a beloved dog, "man's best friend," growing up with a cool young man, and then showed the dog waiting for his owner to return after the man and his friends disappeared with a six-pack of beer. Someone did their research, because the dog waiting worriedly at home was undoubtedly far more effective in reaching young men than showing the ever-anxious (i.e. nagging, annoying, and clueless) mother waiting for their return. Much more effective than the blood-and-gore drunk-driving messages that generally bounce right off the immortal young adult male brain, with their disconnected prefrontal cortex and inherent tendency towards risk-taking. Death is for losers, but disappointing your dog? Unacceptable.

By contrast, the Josh Project's "Hallelujah" video, which aired at the Daytona 500, was designed to reach parents and jolt them into awareness about child drowning.[127] It showed the common thoughts that precede drowning – "I just grabbed the phone for a second," "I didn't hear any splashing" – interspersed with photos of smiling children in water-based scenarios where children typically drown in the United States. Different emotions, different messages, different strategies to reach different audiences. The video would have been even more effective if we had received permission to use Leonard Cohen's "Hallelujah,"[128] because music links directly to emotions, so we settled for visual impact.[129]

It can be daunting, not to mention impossible and outrageously expensive, to reach all the different audiences with effective messages. Use data to identify your key target audiences. Don't try to be an expert in every field. Be an expert in your field and create the best messaging and programs to reach your audience. Be open to collaboration. Every social issue needs a web of resources, support, and messaging working for different targeted audiences.

Another way of thinking about an internalized sustainable change in behavior is to think of it as creating educated instinct. Instinct guides how you react in an emergency or how you approach a potentially dangerous or new situation. When instinct is not educated, the person may or may not make the right decision on how to act. When instinct is educated, it means that the correct behavior has been wired into the brain, overriding what someone may have seen on TV, heard from a friend, or just the primitive response mechanism that has been evolutionarily developed.

Let me give you two examples – of pure instinct and educated instinct – and then we will look at how consistent messages can turn pure instinct into educated instinct.

Pure instinct. When my baby was 3 months old, I was walking her to soothe her and stepped on a wooden block. My feet went flying behind me and I pitched violently forward, landing hard on my knees and elbows on the stone floor. In a split second, with no conscious thought, I had curled myself around her to protect her, with no thought to my personal safety. In such a case, where a split-second decision is called for, we (fortunately) have no hope of overriding the parental instinct to protect or save a child. In most cases, we usually have longer than a split second to act, and those extra seconds can allow educated instinct, or trained behavior, to kick into action.

Educated instinct. When my daughter was young, she woke me at 5.30am, crying hysterically. Emerging out of a deep sleep, I looked over and saw her glowing in the dark. Literally. It took less than a minute for my brain to work through the options and focus on the words "glow stick." She had received a glow stick at a party the night before. I didn't need to know the "why" or "how," I knew she had luminescent chemicals all over her face and body, including her eyes. I leaped out of bed, stuck her under a shower with strict and calm instructions to keep her face pointed into the water for 10 minutes while I dressed, and then headed to the emergency room with the glow stick packaging in hand. I had heard the messages about safety consistently and repetitively since I was a child – in Girl Scouts, in first-aid training, and in health class at school. Rinse the area for 10 minutes in clear, running water and then seek medical attention.

This is educated instinct: when someone is in a traumatic and potentially dangerous situation and, without conscious thought, you are able to reach through your memory to retrieve the correct action and calmly follow through, even if the scenario is different from what you were taught. It is exactly for this reason that first aid and CPR (cardiopulmonary resuscitation) certification requires regular renewal. The information must be drilled in until it is automatically retrieved in panic situations.

Education and training turn pure instinct into educated instinct and can make the difference between a good outcome and a bad outcome. Key to creating educated instinct is consistent messaging. STOP. Don't drink and drive. Fasten your seatbelt. Look both ways before you cross the road. Stop, drop and roll. These are all are public safety messages that work because they are used consistently and repetitively until they infiltrate the brain and become educated instinct. We don't go through a long thought process weighing our options or creating new possible actions when we see a red light. We stop.

When the messages are not consistent, when there is too much playing with words, the messages become diluted and are less likely to turn into educated instinct or actually change behavior. The seemingly harmless manipulation of a message – changing "Swim in areas with lifeguards" to "Swim near a lifeguard," or "Swim near guarded beaches," or "Lifeguards are there for your safety" – make it far less likely that the action will become educated instinct. Wide adoption of the International Open Water Drowning Prevention Guidelines message, "Swim in areas with lifeguards," reiterated consistently and repetitively, begins to create educated instinct.[130] Once you have delivered a consistent message, you can go on to expand on the role of a lifeguard, identify public beaches with lifeguards, and explain that swimming in an area with a lifeguard reduces your chances of drowning to 1 in 18 million. To reinforce the message, always start with, and link back to, your key consistent message: "Swim in areas with lifeguards."

The desire by organizations to differentiate themselves and create unique programming and campaigns poses a major barrier to delivering a consistent message. Intellectual property and jockeying for organizational primacy triumph over behavioral change. This is certainly the case in the drowning prevention field. There is broad agreement on what messages are needed, but there are as many different versions of the messages as there are organizations, which only serves to muddy the water. Progress has been made with Water Safety USA's adoption of the International Guidelines, but widespread adoption has not yet occurred.

One of the most common concerns is that issues are so complex that we cannot possibly boil it down to sound bites for our target audience. The desire to elaborate on the message, preferably at length and in excruciating detail, is less about change and more about our desire to show how much we know about the issue, to establish our credibility, and to be recognized for the hard work that went into developing seemingly simple messages. It is ultimately about ego. Ego may impress but it doesn't change behavior. Aim for simple directive concepts and tell people what to do. Stop, drop and roll. Don't drink and drive. STOP. Once you have their attention and have driven the key message into their brain, then you can elaborate on the details – how to exit a house safely in a fire, assign a designated driver, and obey all traffic signals and look both ways before proceeding carefully.

Be positive when crafting your simple, consistent, and repetitive messages. People are far more likely to internalize the desired behavior if they are positively motivated. Trying to convince people that they want to give up something that brings them joy doesn't work. It is the reason the "Don't drink and drive" campaign has been so successful. People aren't asked to stop drinking; they are asked not to drink *and* drive. The most effective AIDS campaigns don't ask people to stop having sex; they encourage them to use a condom. Doom, gloom, and fear don't sell, and they don't change behavior consistently or sustainably.

4. MEASURE BOTH INTENDED AND UNINTENDED OUTCOMES

Change occurs organically. When you push for change in attitudes and behavior in one area, they often have a ripple effect. Constantly assess and measure each step and, when necessary, change your approach and reassess the process. You may move successfully through the entire process and still need to regroup when you encounter unintended outcomes. Keep the process open and fluid. Test your program on a small population. It is always easier and more cost-effective to start small and scale up than to hurry to market with a great idea and have it fail.

5. CONTINUALLY ASSESS WHETHER THE DESIRED CHANGE IS ACHIEVING YOUR GOAL

Changing behavior is a circular process. If the change you have achieved is not what you expected, ask why and adjust your approach. Sometimes the outcome will be better than you expected, sometimes worse. Be open. As soon as you achieve your goal, set a higher goal and keep going. Creating positive change must be a constant and intentional process because the forces that wish to derail your progress will never rest.

Chapter 5 Worksheet

1. What data exists?
2. What behavioral changes are needed, according to the data?
3. Why should your target audience care about the behavioral change? What is in it for them? (Not dying is not enough of a reason.)
4. What is the one key message you want to communicate? Can the message be understood by someone outside your field?
5. What are your three supporting messages?
6. What are the consequences of not changing?
7. How will you model the desired behavior?
8. Who is your target audience? Who are your collaborators to reach a wider audience with consistent messages?
9. Can you create an educated instinct for the behavior? How would this look? What would it take?

Chapter 6

WHEN POSITIVE MESSAGES AREN'T ENOUGH

At his best, man is the noblest of all animals; separated
from law and justice he is the worst.

Aristotle[131]

The term "utopia" was first created by Sir Thomas More in 1516.[132] Utopia is the idea that perfection can be achieved in society. In utopia, we could issue statements like, "just say no to drugs" or "know how and when to wear a life jacket," and those actions would magically happen. In utopia, we could count on people acting in a way that is beneficial to their well-being, the well-being of those around them, and the well-being of society as a whole. In utopia, all we would need to change behavior would be positive, simple, consistent, and repetitive messages.

We do not live in utopia. Utopia does not exist. Humans and human relationships are imperfect, irrational, and generally messy. Although some people may hope for perfect understanding, world peace, and every day being a good hair day, most of us know that such perfection is elusive. Acknowledging human frailty and complexity, we have created laws and societal norms that provide a framework to rein in and manage the darker and more destructive impulses of humans, and to direct and reinforce societally accepted behaviors. Promoting fear makes for a bleak world. Negative marketing campaigns issuing frightening warnings have dominated influence campaigns of all stripes – social change, public health, public safety, politics, the culture wars.

As we saw in the last chapter, positive messaging and positive reinforcement of desired behavior work, but there are no quick fixes. In this chapter, we will look at structural and punitive options, including laws and negative consequences, that support changes until they become internalized. We identify nontraditional partnerships that can be formed to reinforce positive behavior. Finally, we will identify situations where neither positive nor negative messages can make a difference because the solutions don't address the real problem.

Rules and laws govern every society. Sometimes they are societal norms that are enforced by societal pressures. These include simple manners like saying "please" and "thank you," and expand to attitudes regarding care and respect for children and the elderly. They broaden to encompass society's reaction to discriminatory or antisocial behavior. Societal norms are essentially self-policing; actual laws aren't necessary. Laws are created when a society deems a norm to be so important that it has decided that simple societal disapproval is not enough, and stronger measures are needed to enforce acceptable behavior. These can run the gamut from traffic speed limits, to the regulation of corporate behavior, to prohibiting murder. Laws can also be used as an attempt to club the views of one group into the brains of the entire populace. Laws can be created as a knee-jerk reaction to an event, without thinking through the repercussions of the law or attempting to fix the underlying problems. And, of course, there are the lists of ridiculous laws circulating on the internet, laws which don't make sense outside of the context in which they were enacted. (I may consider moving to Idaho, now that I know it is the only state in the United States that explicitly outlaws cannibalism, and all moose should consider migrating to Alaska, where it is illegal to push a live moose out of an airplane.)[133]

Laws and definitions of justice change over time as societies argue and negotiate what are acceptable behaviors and attitudes. Each society and governing body will weigh considerations differently and reach different conclusions at different times. In the UK, laws impacting child employment began to be passed in 1819. By 1899, only 28 American states had passed child labor laws, but efforts to pass national laws failed repeatedly. It was not until 1938 that Congress passed the national Fair Labor Standards Act which set minimum age requirements for workers. Today, states are weakening the laws again.[134] The United States shamefully remains the only country not to have ratified the United Nations Convention on the Rights of the Child, created in 1989.[135] Child labor continues in many countries, where laws are nonexistent or poorly enforced.

Laws giving votes to women reflect changing societal attitudes. New Zealand led the charge, granting women the right to vote in 1893. The United States followed in 1920, Switzerland belatedly got on board in 1971, and Saudi Arabia finally granted women the vote in 2015. In 2023, the last holdout, the Vatican City, granted women the right to vote in some elections.[136] It took 130 years, and now women's rights are being rolled back, proving once again that social change requires constant pressure.

Laws do not change attitudes; they only restrict or permit specific behaviors. Outlawing child labor does not mean it never occurs if attitudes haven't changed and supporting behaviors aren't regulated. Ending child labor requires us to address the economic necessity that drives child labor and support the societal and cultural frameworks necessary to create a stable and healthy environment for all children. Giving women the right to vote does not erase gender discrimination. Without a broad and concerted campaign to model and reinforce new behaviors, attitudes towards gender equality will never change and there will be constant tension between the laws and existing behavior. Each person and company will do an individual cost–benefit analysis on whether to comply with the new laws or take the risk and not change their behavior. Ideally, laws become unnecessary as attitudes change and new behaviors become accepted and entrenched – just as we hope laws outlawing cannibalism and hurling moose from planes are no longer necessary.

Overwhelming more powerful and well-funded opposition can be achieved if you attack and undermine your competitors' position strategically and have a core of loyal supporters. The Americans won the Revolutionary War, even though the British forces were larger, better funded, and better trained, in part because the Americans knew how to pick their battles and how to undermine defenses and morale using guerrilla tactics.[137] The most important factor in winning the war was the level of popular support; not the majority, but the tipping point of those who cared enough. The tipping point is the number of people who need to take a stand before large-scale social change occurs. Recent research suggests that the tipping point is roughly 25% of people, although some studies suggest a figure as low as 10% or as high as 40%.[138] At no time did more than 45% of American colonists support the Revolutionary War, and at least one third fought for the British, but more people were engaged and fought in the war than in any other conflict in American history.[139] The war was made relevant to enough of the target audience to tip the balance. America also made critically important strategic partnerships with France, Spain, and the Netherlands.[140] Strategic partnerships, defined attacks, and grassroots efforts were made to engage the target audience.

Change never comes easily. We look at cultural norms that were once considered reasonable and fair through the prism of their times and consider many of them to be barbaric at best and deeply unethical and cruel at worst. Even seemingly clear issues, like slavery and torture, thankfully, are considered unethical through our modern prism, although this has not always been the case. Slavery and torture were accepted for thousands of years until activists fought for change. Britain passed the Abolition of Slavery Trade Act in 1807, and the United States passed the 13th Amendment in 1865, but modern-day slavery and human trafficking still exists.[141]

Despite international agreement that torture is unacceptable, debate rages about what constitutes torture. We have moved on from the rack and burning at the stake, but some actors and states are still working to normalize techniques like waterboarding and isolation. We have difficulty agreeing on anything. Some ethicists argue that certain practices, like genocide, are morally wrong no matter what your prism, but even then, the definition of genocide is subject to emotionally engaging marketing. There is a theory of ethical relativism which "holds that morality is relative to the norms of one's culture."[142] The idea is that perceptions of right and wrong change, not through chance, but through the intentional reframing of issues within current cultural frameworks. In other words, everything seems normal until activists push for change. Even ethics are marketed.

To create positive change in society, we need to address societal norms that act as barriers to the change. Each society, or sub-group within a society, will have different viewpoints. For change to be successful, communicate change by framing the issue in a way that appeals to your different audiences. The starting point is always positive, simple, consistent, and repetitive messages, but the nuances in language to explain and expand are important. Demonstrating how effectively corporations use marketing, the term "climate change" was determined to be more benign than "global warming" by the fossil fuel industry because "change" seems inevitable and slow, whereas "warming" is something the average person can feel and compels them to take action. Seemingly simple changes in wording by the fossil fuel industry has translated into decades of lost time.[143] An interesting study showed that addressing climate change became a priority for both liberals and conservatives if the issue was described in a way that created a sense of moral urgency based on their personal beliefs.[144] A few different words, a shift in emphasis, and "not my issue" becomes "this is my issue." This willingness to look at an issue through someone else's eyes rarely occurs. Instead, we continue to pound home our ideas and values against an increasingly resistant audience who dig in and become more committed to rejecting change.

The level of responsibility differs by the individual, the family, the community, and the country. As a nation, the United States tends towards the fierce defense of individual rights and state rights, although what constitutes patriotism remains divisive. In much of Asia, the collective rights of the family and societal units are deemed more important culturally and historically than the rights of the individual. Understand the culture before you begin drafting and lobbying for laws, so you can frame your arguments to lawmakers and the public appropriately. Market the change within the cultural context.

No matter what the culture, laws that attempt to change behavior without adequately explaining the need for behavior change or providing alternative behaviors tend to be less effective. Speed limits for traffic are a perfect example of laws that redirect behavior without addressing the attitudes or underlying cause of the behavior. Road accidents are a leading cause of death globally. The data shows that as speed limits go up, traffic fatalities go up. The state of Illinois used data to create targeted programs for at-risk drivers, teens. The Graduated Driver Licensing program has reduced fatalities in teenage drivers by 50% since it was introduced.[145] The threat of a ticket or traffic school keeps many drivers within 10 mph (16 km/h) of the limit, but there is still a major disconnect between the law and the public's willingness to obey the speed limit. Speed limits are perceived as a nuisance and killjoy that are imposed on the public and are often treated more as a suggestion. Anecdotally, I can confirm that it is deeply disconcerting to be driving a powerful Audi at 90 mph (145 km/h) on the French autoroute and see a Renault Clio with four nuns onboard coming up behind like I was standing still. Clearly, they had an assurance of safety from a higher authority than my mere air bags and seat belts.

Change is easier with help, especially help that brings different perspectives. For-profit products can promote and support behavior change. A billboard that makes drinking water out of the humidity in the air in a region with little potable water.[146] A fun buoyancy aid shaped like a shark fin that helps stabilize children as they are learning to swim under supervision without limiting their arm and leg movements.[147] A straw that filters harmful bacteria and viruses out of water, turning unsafe water into safe drinking water.[148] Products that reduce dependency on fossil fuels and address the issue of irregular or scarce access to conventional electricity, like solar-powered cell-phone chargers or solar-powered light created from a recycled plastic bottle and chlorinated water.[149] Products developed by people motivated to solve a problem following a personal experience, like the brightly colored float that swimmers can wear in open water so they are visible to boaters and other powered watercraft.[150] Innovations using resources in new and totally different ways, like the cell-phone app that acts as an ultrasound for pregnant women in Uganda, or an app that can detect malaria using a light sensor on a cell phone.[151] Many of these inventors are classified as "social entrepreneurs," a person who establishes an enterprise with the aim of solving social problems or effecting social change. Social entrepreneurs are often ideal strategic partners because they are focused on the same issues, just from a different angle.

For-profit companies can become good partners. Corporate social responsibility (CSR) refers to a company assessing and taking responsibility for its impact on the environment and social welfare. Some companies rally around an official chosen cause, while others encourage employees to take work time to volunteer for the cause of their choice. Still others donate time, materials or expertise. The concept of corporate social responsibility first began during the 1950s and took off during the 1970s. The concept has evolved to the point that many companies attribute their CSR with producing happier and better employees, and approach CSR as a desirable benefit to the community rather than just the bottom line, although the bottom line benefits as well. The concept of "goodwill" in accounting represents the value of a company's brand name and appears as an asset on the balance sheet. Such goodwill is increased by positive public perception of a company's name and reputation, which can be burnished by a vibrant CSR program, although pressure and marketing by some groups is forcing corporations to retreat from CSR and other social impact initiatives.

An energy company desiring extensive operations in Vietnam wished to be viewed as a good corporate citizen. After learning that child drowning is an epidemic in flood-prone Vietnam, the firm decided to provide children in grades 1 to 5 with specially made school backpacks that became life jackets if they fell into water.[152] Given that many children in Vietnam travel on or near water to get to school, the life jacket/backpack reinforced the importance of children attending school while recognizing that the journey to and from school can be dangerous. In the first three years of the program, the company delivered over 14,000 life jacket/backpacks. They partnered with Swim Vietnam and Hue Help to conduct water safety awareness training in conjunction with delivering the life jacket/backpacks at six primary schools in Binh Dinh. To support local businesses, the company worked with a local registered supplier who invented the special life jacket/backpacks. They coordinated with local authorities and the Department of Education and Training, with company staff volunteering their time. The energy company subsequently was sold and rebranded after accusations of genocide, providing a cautionary tale as to the necessity of identifying potential social washing.[153] Save the Children later stepped up and distributed floating backpacks.[154]

Identify an ideal corporate partner based on mutual gain. Develop a strong sales pitch that explains in financial terms why partnering with your organization or cause is a good business decision, and then sell your story. Knock on doors and keep your foot in the doors until they agree to hear your pitch. For instance, the two biggest producers of swim diapers are Procter & Gamble and Kimberly-Clark. If your interest is introducing swim lessons for children, the American Academy of Pediatrics recommended age of 1 year old creates a strong positive correlation between more young children in the water and an instant increase in sales of swim diapers.[155] Even better if your program is in an area where the companies have employees. Less obvious partners that would benefit from having more children becoming comfortable in the water include water parks; swimming pool and equipment manufacturers; swimsuit, goggle and swim cap manufacturers; and the chemical companies that produce pool chemicals. When a corporation will be an immediate or future beneficiary of your business model, think of them as a potential strategic partner. Doing good feels good, but it is even better to do good in a way that is effective, sustainable, and financially viable.

There will be times when you identify competition in the form of a product or company that needs to be minimized or eliminated. Sometimes that competition will be inadvertent – they are filling a demand that no one understands is dangerous or has been identified as less than optimal over time. The bane of my drowning prevention existence is inflatable armbands, also known as water wings. As is the case with many products, they were born of good intentions but have outlived their useful life and need to be permanently retired. The first inflatable armband was introduced in London in 1907 when swimming became part of the school curriculum and parents became more concerned about drowning. They appeared on Californian beaches in 1931 and in Germany in 1964. The problem is, if something inflates, it also deflates. Putting inflatable armbands on a child gives both the child and the parent a false sense of security. It limits the mobility of the child, it is easy for a child to forget they are not wearing their armbands and jump into a pool, it takes no time for an armband to slip off a slender arm, inflatable armbands can develop a slow leak that you don't notice until it is too late, and neither armbands nor children stand little chance in the open ocean where a child can be knocked down by a rogue wave or pulled in by a rip current. Plus, their environmental impact is terrible. Inflatable armbands need to go.

Many products, or components of products, seemed like a good idea at the time, but research and society's perceptions change. Coca-Cola contained cocaine until 1903.[156] It wasn't just Coca-Cola; cough medicine and tonics laced with cocaine were regularly sold by peddlers and drugstores. Laudanum, which is opium, was widely used in Victorian England, including liberally dosing children with Godfrey's Cordial (marketed as Mother's Friend) to keep them quiet.[157] At the time, cocaine and opium were thought to be safe. The lesson? Don't storm the barricades assuming that a company is intentionally doing harm. Understand the context of the product, what has changed, and what new information is available. Even better, approach a company with an idea that will allow them to continue or even expand their business while removing the now dangerous product. Of course, if they willfully continue to do harm, change strategy immediately.

If you are determined to eliminate a product, think through the repercussions. Identify well-researched and well-marketed alternative products and behaviors. More children will drown if you simply eliminate inflatable armbands without providing and marketing alternatives and encouraging behavior change, like staying within arm's reach of young children and weak swimmers and using only U.S. Coast Guard-approved flotation devices. If everyone throws their inflatable armbands in the garbage (because they aren't recyclable), they will almost certainly end up in landfills or in the Great Pacific Garbage Patch where the plastic will break into tinier and tinier pieces, which is extremely harmful to both marine life and humans when it enters the food chain. Before you ask people to toss, flush, or dump a product, work through how you are going to eliminate the problem permanently. Partner with organizations who can help to eliminate and dispose of the product safely.[158] Don't just shift the problem to another group or issue.

Companies invest a huge amount of capital in each product, including research and development, marketing, manufacturing, and materials inventory. Business decisions are influenced by attitudes regarding profits, shareholder return, executive pay, and the too rarely discussed egos and personality types of those in the top positions. Remember, humans are rarely rational, and humans run companies. It can take a concerted effort of several strategic interests working together to convince corporations of the need to change. Nestlé's exploitative marketing of baby formula in Africa in the 1970s, when the water used to mix the formula was unsafe, made it all the way to Senate Hearings and the World Health Organization before a new set of marketing rules were issued.[159] Fast forward 50 years, and Nestlé is back in the news over again misrepresenting both baby formula and water rights.[160] When we fail to address the root causes of problems, they often resurface. Ask the whys.

Don't get discouraged. Whatever your cause, look for success stories. Revlon now publishes an ingredients policy, which may or may not be in response to pressure by the Breast Cancer Fund and the Environmental Working Group.[161] Greenpeace, World Wildlife Fund, and other green groups lobbied Asia Pulp & Paper for decades on deforestation, which ultimately led to the New York Declaration on Forests signed by more than 150 governments, businesses, and nonprofits at the United Nations Climate Summit in 2014.[162] Nike was targeted for allowing suppliers in poor countries to abuse and exploit workers and has taken action to change their image, with mixed success.[163] When you do succeed, be gracious. Give credit where credit is due. Acknowledge the efforts of all parties and set the groundwork for ongoing mutually beneficial strategic partnerships. Greenpeace created a wonderful thank-you video for Kimberly-Clark when they reached an agreement on protecting old-growth forests because thank you is always in style.[164]

There will be situations where neither positive nor negative messages can make a difference because the solutions don't address the real problem. Don't assume you know the answers. Look at the underlying reasons for noncompliance – they may be surprising.

Girls in East Africa were not going to school. On the surface, a lack of books or uniforms, attitudes towards girls, or transportation were possible culprits. While these were certainly contributing factors, by peeling back the layers, researchers discovered that a key issue was that when girls had their period, they were far more likely to skip school to avoid embarrassment and inconvenience. Girls couldn't afford sanitary napkins. Once they were provided with menstrual cups, attendance immediately improved. Menstrual cups provide a cost-effective and long-term solution to keeping girls in school. The girls knew they wanted to go to school and they understood the importance of the messages they were receiving, they just needed help on what would have appeared to be an unrelated issue. One subsequent evaluation showed that cash transfers and menstrual cups led to a lower rate of sexually transmitted infections (STIs), risky sexual behaviors, and lower school dropout rates, although another study showed a reduction in STIs but not in dropout rates. Unintentional outcomes still showed positive change.[165]

Understanding power dynamics is key when dealing with an issue where wealth has reached such a level that it is relevant only in terms of being used as an expression of power and influence.

We have seen a shift in preventing wildlife poaching from unsuccessfully pleading with the public to save majestic animals to working towards cutting the demand for products from poached animals and making those products socially undesirable. There is still a long way to go on these education programs, time that endangered animals may not have. Scarcity drives up prices and fuels demand for those who crave exclusivity, putting endangered animals at greater risk. It is the same mindset that kept Harley-Davidson motorcycles selling at or above their list price in the 1990s.[166] Demand surged, supply could not keep up, and it was frankly comical to watch all the Masters of the Universe when they realized their power and money could not get them a Harley-Davidson any faster than anyone else on the waiting list. The scarcity drove purchase prices up to $15,000 over the normal price and made owning a Harley-Davidson an expression of power, influence, and wealth, beyond the usual culture of freedom and rebelliousness against the establishment. The allure of power and social status should never be underestimated.

Follow the money chain to the point of real influence and understand how those further down the chain are being influenced or coerced. A ranger in South Africa explained to me that one of the biggest issues they have with poachers is the fact that the poachers themselves are viewed as a disposable resource by the money further up the chain, generally organized crime. Every time a poacher is killed or captured, they are easily replaced because, while the money made by poachers is a tiny fraction of what an animal is worth on the black market, it is significantly above what they could make in a regular job in communities where unemployment rates hover around 27% and the average annual income of a Black household is around $7,000.[167] The poachers are simply pawns in a bigger game, often driven by economic necessity to support their families. Not to say that all poachers are good people or not at fault, but if you follow the money, you find the real culprits – those fueling the demand and those providing the supply. Positive and negative behaviors are driven by a range of needs and desires.

We often see political and corporate interests using marketing techniques to deflect attention from laws and policies that benefit a smaller group at the expense of the general population. These groups and individuals are adept at creating hysteria over issues while quietly pursuing their own agenda. Bait and switch is a popular tactic, as is the selective use of data and facts. Bullying. Peer pressure. Manipulation of public information. Financial incentives – both legal and illegal. All are widely used. Don't be diverted. Do opposition research. Follow the money. Ask the whys. Check your emotions at the door. Keep calm. When you are passionate about an issue, it is easy for someone to wind you up and set you walking in one direction while they quietly move an entire army behind your flailing arms and impassioned speeches. Understand your own hot spots and triggers; they are your greatest weakness. Make an effort to understand how the other side thinks. Search out people, organizations, and news outlets that regularly embrace opposite viewpoints. Study the root of those beliefs and how they are effectively marketed. Understand that different people respond to different emotions, actions, and verbal cues. Don't assume that the arguments that work for you will work for everyone.

The inability to listen, understand, and engage opposing points of view has the same outcome as selling cod liver oil in an unheated shack: a few of the party faithful feeling self-righteous as they shiver. For widespread change, develop a mutually appealing program equivalent to caviar and champagne on a yacht in the Mediterranean. Undermine any apathy in the population you are trying to convince or change. Apathy results from being lulled into a false sense of security through effective marketing assuring you that everything is all right. Don't worry, be happy. Denial is a comfortable state. Look at how many refused to believe that the unsinkable *Titanic* could sink, even as it sank. You need a compelling reason to convince people to man the lifeboats and paddle for a better outcome. Passion and commitment are wonderful drivers for change, as long as they don't overwhelm your common sense and ability to work pragmatically and collaboratively.

Finally, money drives every issue. Money on its own is just an easy way of facilitating transactions, but it symbolizes so much more. Freedom. Independence. Power. Prestige. Self-worth. There are some who reject economic binds to society, but they are the exception, not the rule. Their very refusal to engage on an economic level is a form of self-actualization. Their repudiation of money fulfills them. Many of our statutes revolve around money to some extent or another. The penalty for breaking the written laws is economic, whether fines or imprisonment, which deprive someone of the ability to earn or spend money. Our unwritten laws of social conduct are enforced by economic censure to some extent. Self-expression and acceptance are often manifested in tangible goods – clothing, electronics, houses, cars, watches. It is not only wealthy societies that have such symbols. Electricity, a bicycle, access to water, books for school, school fees, livestock, regular meals; even the basic necessities for living can be translated into external symbols of well-being.

Money makes the world go round, and makes research, data, communication campaigns, products, staffing, and support for change possible – or, as Nelson Mandela said, "Money won't create success, the freedom to make it will."[168]

Chapter 6 Worksheet

1. What positive messaging is currently effective?
2. What audiences are responding to the positive messages? What audiences are ignoring the positive messages?
3. Describe the social norms around the behavior.
4. What laws exist that impact the behavior?
5. Follow the money – who are the beneficiaries of the current system?
6. What for-profit corporations benefit from the current system?
7. What for-profit corporations would benefit from changing the system and from the new behaviors?
8. What success stories exist around the new behavior?
9. What negative or warning messages are needed? What audience do you need to test these messages on?

HOW TO GET FUNDING

The importance of money flows from it being a link between the present and the future.

John Maynard Keynes[169]

You have an idea. You are determined to make the world a better place. Now, you just need the funding.

Many have gone before you with brilliant ideas, and many have failed. It is hard to get data on the number of nonprofits that fail because many just fade into obscurity. Around 30% of nonprofits fail within 10 years, 77% don't have a leadership transition plan, and 20% of the largest nonprofits don't have a business plan.[170] For-profit businesses also struggle to survive, with 65% failing during the first 10 years.[171] No matter how you slice the numbers, launching and sustaining a viable operation is difficult.

There are many ways businesses can fail – bad ideas, misjudging the market, superior competition, poor leadership, or lack of infrastructure. There is one certain way to fail – money. The fastest way to go out of business, no matter what your business, is not having or managing money effectively.[172] Money is the link between your idea having both a present and a future.

Perhaps just hearing the words "business" and "money" left you thinking you could skip this chapter and focus on more meaningful ways of saving the world. After all, your goal is clear, your motives are altruistic, and your cause is just, therefore the money will flow. Wrong attitude. Money matters.

In this chapter, we will examine the role of money, the power of money, the motivating power of money, and the relative worth conferred by money.

THE ROLE OF MONEY

I believe that the single biggest barrier to positive change in the world is our conflicted attitude towards money. Not money itself, but how we talk and feel about money. Every country and culture has its own language and societal norms around accumulating, spending, and sharing money. These beliefs are not comfortably held and are frequently at the root of armed conflict and more subtle forms of engagement. Beliefs about money form the underpinnings for class systems, political systems, attitudes towards social welfare, gender equality, access to education, employment, social status, and the very value of human life, including whether some lives are perceived as being worth more than other lives. We use money to assign worth.

All these attitudes ignore the fact that money is simply the conduit through which goods and services are funneled. Money facilitates transactions, which are determined to be desirable or undesirable based on our perceptions, which are influenced by marketing. Money is an integral part of marketing because it eases the facilitation and consummation of exchanges. We no longer have to haul a chicken to market to trade for wool. Money facilitates marketing, but it is the marketing of the value of goods, services, and behaviors that has the true power, not the money that facilitates the exchange.

A product or service is marketed to you, and you hand over the amount of money that has been determined by both buyer and seller to be a fair exchange. Note that both the buyer and the seller are involved in determining whether an exchange is fair. In a truly competitive market, any product, experience, service, or level of influence must be perceived by the buyer to be worth the investment of money and behavior change or there won't be an exchange. How the price is set is heavily influenced by marketing. A Bugatti La Voiture Noire sells for about $12 million.[173] A Nissan Versa is $16,755.[174] Both will get you from point A to B, admittedly at a very different speed, but the price of each car is reflective of successfully marketing emotional engagement, creating either the tug of scarcity and prestige or the allure of affordability and good gas mileage.

THE POWER OF MONEY

There is equal danger in attributing too much power to money and not enough power to money. Attributing too much power assumes that if you just throw enough money at a problem, it will be solved. The focus on data-driven solutions developed, in part, because we know that money is not enough; we are looking for proof that money invested in programs gives a good return on investment. The greater danger lies in underestimating the power of money. This manifests itself in becoming overreliant on volunteers to make up for a lack of paid staff, deterring business-minded people from entering the field by penalizing them financially, being overly zealous in minimizing overhead costs as a percentage of overall operating costs, and not placing enough value on attracting and nurturing a financial base.

There is a continuing bias within the social change and non-profit communities that they are somehow above financial concerns. Worse is the idea that it is somehow noble and desirable not to place any emphasis on money. This bias is supported, to some extent, by the personality type that gravitates towards the social change field; the personality type that does not measure worth in purely monetary terms and may even dismiss monetary rewards as undesirable or unimportant. As Albert Camus said, "It's a kind of spiritual snobbery that makes people think they can be happy without money."[175] Unfortunately, this disregard for money by one segment of the population has allowed another segment to accumulate ever greater amounts of money, along with the power and influence that accompany wealth, which then allows them to set the agenda for policies and social change.

By refusing to understand and leverage the power of money, we lose the power to effect change. By refusing to quantify the value of social change in monetary terms, we hand power to forces that work against those changes. By monetarily undervaluing the work done by those in the social change fields, we cede control to the people who insist on having their value recognized and agendas promoted, often at the expense of wider society. We are all partly to blame for today's social ills because we have refused to fight for our own worth, and the worth of our ideas, on the societally established playing field where money denotes value.

THE MOTIVATING POWER OF MONEY

We don't all need to be motivated by money or aspire to accumulate great wealth, but we do need to understand that throughout most of recorded history, money has conferred value and power. Our society has determined that money is a relative measure of worth, and that worth is reflected in salaries and operating budgets. When significant sums of money are spent on creating and powering AI, providing esoteric financial services, and developing industry subsidies, their value is implied to society. When that money is diverted from addressing climate breakdown, eradicating poverty, implementing common-sense gun control, reducing violence against women, or conserving wildlife, their diminished value to society is implied. By ignoring this reality, and not building financial strength into your business model, you minimize both the importance and the impact of the work you do. Stop accepting the current perception that tech entrepreneurs and bankers deserve the big bucks, and change-makers and those directly improving society should be happy with peanuts. You can, and should, challenge that long-standing status quo.

There are professions that have declared themselves to be of high financial value – private equity investors, investment bankers, professional athletes, tech professionals, lobbyists, some entertainers, and executives in certain industries, to name just a few. These professions often attract a personality type that places a high value on a financial reward that reflects their perceived self-worth, even if it is out of sync with their relative contribution to society, or even damaging to society. The argument for high salaries is usually tied to their revenue-producing potential and perceived (marketed) contribution to the global economy. In terms of benefiting society, it is hard to justify paying a professional football player $61.3 million but paying a teacher only $58,603 a year, below the median wage of $59,436.[176] Research shows a good teacher can increase a student's lifelong income by $266,000.[177] Doing the math, a 40-year teaching career with 25 students each year works out at $266,000,000 more income circulating in the economy. Call me biased and cranky, but beyond tribal loyalty and entertainment, professional football players do not benefit society. The big winners are the 32 National Football League (NFL) team owners, to the tune of $18.6 billion a year in revenue from a fresh infusion of cash from private equity, all while they further increase their wealth with help from their nonprofit tax status.[178] Meanwhile, the nurses who care for players with concussions have a median salary of $86,070, despite being named the most trusted profession by the public for 22 consecutive years.[179] We don't make decisions based solely on logic; we base decisions on emotions, which are influenced on attitudes and behaviors, which are influenced by marketing. Those who value money award themselves even when they fail. During the 2008 financial crisis, which essentially took $70,00 from every American's pocket, $1.6 billion in bailout money went to banking executives – the guys who caused the problem in the first place.[180] CEO salaries increased 1,322% from 1978 to 2019, while the compensation for the typical worker grew by just 18% during the same period.[181] Worse, purchasing power has not shifted during that time, so American workers essentially haven't received a single raise in 41 years.[182] High salaries are not based on rational economic analysis. The salaries in such professions reflects the perceived and well-marketed self-worth of the recipients and those who benefit by association.

We contribute to the inequality in perceived value by not understanding the financial playing field. That said, we cannot and should not expect salaries to change simply because we change our perceived value of a profession. The personality types would shift to follow the money, and it is frightening to imagine "greed is good" Gordon Gecko teaching kindergarten.[183]

Note: Individuals who are limited by lack of education, poverty, discrimination, lack of opportunity, and other barriers to advancement, or who are working in some of the most dangerous or poorly paid jobs, have little or no bargaining power either on their own or collectively and should be excluded from any assumption that their lack of economic or marketing clout can be easily remedied or is in any way their fault. The onus to improve their situation is not the responsibility of the 17% of the global population living in extreme poverty; it is a moral, ethical, and financial stability issue for our entire society. When the United States has more low-paid jobs than any other country in the OECD, over 25% of all jobs, it is a problem of a growing imbalance of wealth and power, not a problem that individuals or specific professions can resolve on their own. Shifting blame and responsibility for poverty to the individual has been marketed effectively for long enough. Only changes in government policies, tax codes, subsidies, and corporate governance can significantly alter the status quo.

THE RELATIVE WORTH CONFERRED BY MONEY

When a person or organization does not value their self-worth in monetary terms, society assigns a lower value to their contribution. Salaries in the nonprofit and social change world are consistently below those in the for-profit world, contributing to a public perception that the work being done by nonprofits is not as valuable. From the CEO on down, there is an enormous differential in pay. The median salary for a CEO at one of the top 350 for-profit firms in the United States is $27.8 million vs. $2 million average for the 23 CEOs in the nonprofit world that make over $1 million, a 92% penalty.[184] If you carve out highly paid health and university system CEOs, the average pay for 426 nonprofits was $166,996, a 99.3% penalty.[185] The average for-profit salary is $59,384 but only $48,688 for a nonprofit, an 18% penalty.[186] The percentage differences aren't exact, as it is difficult to find comparable data in one location, but the distance between salaries is well-documented in many studies. Nonprofit employees are paid (valued) less. The nonprofit and nongovernmental organization (NGO) fields also rely heavily on free labor in the form of volunteers. The social change community must challenge themselves to create financially viable models for change, including paying salaries that are competitive with for-profit enterprises.

Salaries are not the only indicator of worth or value. The most common way of assessing whether an organization is successful is by measuring its results. For-profit organizations have established accounting methodologies to measure results, including profits, dividends, and return on investment. Value is measured in monetary terms. It is difficult to measure the value of social change in monetary terms, in part because such accounting methodologies do not exist. We are left defending the paying of competitive salaries (overheads) which, in theory, diminish the amount spent on programs, even though hiring the right talent and giving them the resources to develop, test, and widely implement effective programs would yield a solid return on investment in terms of measurable change.

Nonprofits and NGOs tend to rely heavily on volunteers to make up for the shortfall in talent due to smaller budgets for staff and lower salaries overall. Volunteering has an important place in our society. Volunteering removes the transactional dynamic from human relations and makes us more empathetic. Volunteering allows people to use skills and explore interests that they may not be able to use in other parts of their lives. Volunteering provides a valuable form of fulfillment that is different from working for a paycheck. It is a distinct mindset and one that is rightfully valued. However, organizations that are forced to operate using predominantly volunteers are doomed to function at a lower level of effectiveness. Imagine if hospitals had to rely predominantly on volunteers, wondering if medical technicians, housekeepers, and food service workers would volunteer their time. I doubt volunteers would be beating down the door to clean up the blood, guts, and vomit. Organizations need a solid and competitively compensated core staff in order to make a difference. Attracting and retaining volunteers is an important part of a successful strategy, but it shouldn't be the primary strategy.

In my twenties, I volunteered at Northwestern Hospital, a large teaching hospital in Chicago. I will never forget the first volunteer appreciation banquet I attended. The CEO of the hospital thanked the packed ballroom of volunteers for donating over one million unpaid hours of our time. One million hours of cuddling babies, delivering flowers, transporting patients, manning the information desk, and any other number of jobs which meant that medical and housekeeping professionals could focus on providing quality medical care to the patients. One million volunteer hours had a positive impact on the bottom line, both financially and in terms of the effectiveness of the hospital, something the nonprofit hospital management wished to quantify to recognize the value. One million hours was impressive, but imagine if the CEO had taken it to the next level and put the contribution in monetary terms. Even if those volunteer hours were paid at the minimum wage of the time, they would still work out to roughly $3.8 million in value. Now, $3,800,000 has greater perceived value than one million hours. We equate money with value.

There is precedence. "Goodwill" on a balance sheet is an established mechanism for measuring something intangible in a for-profit business. If we can measure the intangible value of a name or reputation, we can develop protocols for measuring the value of social change. We can re-evaluate how investors are rewarded in terms of the tax implications if we want to influence behavior and drive more people to invest in social change. Donations to nonprofits are tax-deductible in some situations, but are negligible compared to taxation rules regarding dividends, short-term and long-term capital gains, and losses that contribute to for-profit business success.

Changing the status quo can also be achieved through social intervention. Social intervention is a social science theory for creating "programs designed to deliver social benefits and develop human capital of specific target groups" with an objective of socio-economic development.[187] Social intervention builds on people's desire for others to think highly of them. We want people to like us and approve of us.[188] The goal of social intervention is to change society through "the dissemination of intentional change strategies" – another way of describing social marketing.[189] Provide people with information about how others around them are behaving to encourage changes in behavior. This technique leverages and creates social norms, "perceived, informal and mostly unwritten rules that define acceptable and appropriate actions within a group or community."[190] Companies go green, use renewable energy, support diversity, give back to local communities, or support local initiatives. Notice that companies also spend significant advertising money talking about how they are doing good. They want credit for following social norms. The changes in behavior come about through a combination of external social pressure and an internal analysis of how change would affect the bottom line. To be competitive and keep increasing their bottom line, companies change their business model. When companies and the executives don't see a benefit to their bottom line or a personal benefit, it doesn't matter how much social pressure exists, they will brazen it through and capture short-term profits. Never let up on the pressure. Pivot when existing techniques are no longer effective because social norms have changed or the competition have altered their strategy.

Devaluing one way of doing business does not automatically increase the value of alternative ways of doing business. There are many for-profit companies that offer innovation, a good return on investment, satisfying work opportunities, competitive salaries, and goods and services that benefit many people globally. We want to nurture both for-profit and nonprofit enterprises which support the public good. We also want to crush the damaging competition out of existence.

There is no one right way. Humans are complex. Individuals value different things. They want different lifestyles. They measure happiness and personal success in different ways. There are as many people who not only choose but are happy with few outward trappings of wealth as there are people who pursue and prefer those trappings. Warren Buffett, billionaire investor and one of the richest men in the world, maintains a lifestyle that hasn't changed much since before he made his billions. He still lives in the modest house he bought in 1958.[191] Paul Allen, billionaire co-founder of Microsoft, owns a $100 million yacht, two sports teams, a few museums, and a MiG-29 Russian fighter jet, among other things.[192] Different people, different lifestyle choices. It shows amazing hubris to assume that everyone wants what we want. It is also deeply insulting to assume that someone living happily on the median income of $67,521 a year is living a less important or fulfilling life than someone earning $226.9 billion.[193]

Change won't happen by sitting quietly by and hoping someone notices your good work and tosses a few coins in your tin cup. It won't happen by creating a market pitch that focuses only on "doing good" without a solid financial argument. It won't happen by feeling the warm glow of moral superiority that you are somehow a better person because you are doing work that contributes to society while being underpaid or unpaid. It will only happen when you value your contribution, demonstrate a competitive return on investment, and insist on salaries that are competitive with the for-profit world. As Joe Biden said in 2013: "Don't tell me what you value, show me your budget and I will tell you what you value."[194]

It is wrong when marketing worsens the human condition rather than enhances the human condition. It is wrong when shame and despair are marketed more effectively than hope. The widening gap in wealth is creating a society where most people are struggling to stay afloat. This trend will continue until people decide that their lives and children and work are worthwhile. It isn't a new fight. In 1942, Heinrich Himmler, the head of the German SS and the man most responsible for putting Hitler's genocidal plans into action, said, "Whether nations live in prosperity or starve to death interests me only insofar as we need them as slaves for our culture."[195] Refuse to be a slave to someone else's culture. Understand what is being done and fight the influence of money with money.

Chapter 7 Worksheet

1. What is your current attitude towards money? Write down the first 10 words you think of when you hear the word "money." (This can be done individually or by the entire organization.)
2. Make two columns, "positive" and "negative." Assign your attitudes towards money to the columns. What do your attitudes tell you? Do you have an adversarial relationship with money? A positive relationship? A conflicted relationship?
3. What goods or services does money buy that is directly related to the change you want to see?
4. How do your current attitudes about money interfere with that change?
5. What is the monetary value of the goods, services, or change you want to see? Don't fall back on "better for humanity"; quantify your argument with positive examples (e.g., What is the financial benefit of stopping and potentially reversing the breakdown of the climate on individuals/nations? What is the cost of medical treatment for unhealthy behaviors?).
6. What is the cost of not changing? Who is benefitting from the status quo? Quantify your examples with negative examples (e.g., What is the cost of not addressing the climate emergency? What is the cost of each nonfatal drowning?).
7. If you have volunteers, make a spreadsheet and track the hours and assign a monetary value to the work. Look at job search boards to find current for-profit pay rates. What is the monetary value of the volunteers in your organization?
8. Compare the salaries of employees in your nonprofit organization to comparable positions in the for-profit world. What is the difference? If you can't make up the difference

financially, are there benefits, perks, or nonmonetary ways of recognizing employees to make up the difference until you can increase salaries? Can you market those compensatory rewards as a marketing/recruitment tool?

9. Ask your board of directors for a full bio. What are you missing in terms of tapping into their talents? Where is your board missing expertise? Can you recruit board members to fill the expertise gaps?

10. Make a list of all the competitors for behavior change. Download their annual reports and follow the money. Where are they spending? What are their financial priorities? What financial priorities can you target to market your change?

Chapter 8

CONTROL THE MONEY, CONTROL THE CHANGE

If we command our wealth, we shall be rich and free. If
our wealth commands us, we are poor indeed.

Edmund Burke[196]

You can't measure happiness, or so the saying goes. Happiness is a state of mind, an emotion, a perception. What makes one person happy may have no meaning for someone else. We tend to apply the same mentality to social change and improving the human condition, to our detriment. There is a common plea of "How can you put a price on a life?" or the environment, or wildlife, or reducing intolerance, or freedom. In a philosophical sense it is true, we cannot put a price on our ideals, but we routinely assign a relative value to our ideals by deciding who gets money and how money is spent. The decision can be active, by directing the spending, or it can be passive, by ceding the decision-making to others.

What stories do the following budgets tell you? The budget for country A shows the largest expenditure in retirement security (21%), retirement healthcare (14%), interest payments (13%), health (13%), and defense (13%).[197] Country B's budget shows education (15%), social security and employment (15%), health and sanitation (8%), and agriculture, forestry, and water (9%) as the top four priorities.[198] City C devotes 32% of their budget to building public safety, 31% to clean and healthy communities, and 16% to "prioritizing our youth."[199] City D sets general financing requirements (47%) and infrastructure services (20%) as predominant budgetary priorities.[200] Lung cancer is the cause of 23% of cancer deaths, but funding for lung cancer research ranks third, attracting 8.2% of funding.[201] As we saw in Chapter 7, the money tells a story: "Don't tell me what you value, show me your budget and I will tell you what you value."[202] Use this quote as a regular filter when assessing the budgets of collaborators and competitors, and when building your budget.

It is equally interesting to look at how budgets are communicated and marketed to the public. Baltimore won a Distinguished Budget Presentation Award.[203] Los Angeles produces a range of reports with few number- and text-intensive details and easy-to-understand graphics in summary format.[204] Only a few years ago, New York City's budget was 291 pages of text-thick words and numbers that looked as if it was produced in the days of punch cards and mainframe computers. They have upgraded, but it is still hard to get the big picture.[205] Chicago doesn't attach percentages to the graphs depicting the money spent on general government and public safety.[206] They stick with numbers, essentially obscuring how the relative value of the numbers fit into the big picture. The numbers tell a story. How the numbers are communicated (marketed) to the public tells a story.

In this chapter, we will examine how to eliminate the emotion from our quantification of change while simultaneously leveraging emotion in our communication of change.

If you sell a shirt, you know the sales price and the production cost. Calculating profit and other markers of financial success are simple equations defined by established accounting rules with significant cultural and accounting leeway for failing and trying again, as long as profits are consistently produced and shareholders are satisfied. Risk is rewarded and being overly cautious leaves organizations behind the competition. Measuring the success of social or behavioral change is more ephemeral and heavily skewed towards avoiding risk by calling out faults in research and acknowledging that there is no perfect answer. While this is a desirable intellectual standard, it leads to a whole lot of good ideas languishing on a shelf or behind academic paywalls, while for-profit ideas are out there "swinging for the fences," as Coca-Cola proudly explained (marketed) about the New Coke debacle.[207]

For-profit companies take a chance on what might work and routinely try and fail, heavily influencing attitudes and behaviors. Meanwhile, researchers and scientists list everything that could possibly be wrong with their research, dwell on the caveats, and hunker down in a defensive crouch debating the details, while little changes in the real world. The very intellectual curiosity and skepticism that drives talented researchers is used against them. Think of how often you have heard a climate denier say that not all scientists agree about human-driven global warming. The fossil fuel industry has successfully marketed completely unrelated events (e.g., meteors causing an ice age and natural variations in climate over millions of years) and the cautious caveats of scientists, instead of the reality that 97% of currently publishing climate scientists agree that human behavior is warming our planet, and most of it has occurred in the last 15 years because of the unrestrained burning of fossil fuels.[208] Put another way, if I give you a 3% chance of living if you don't take action, and a 97% chance of living if you do take action, are you really betting on the 3%? Probably not, unless it is very effectively marketed.

The culture of questioning and challenging keeps researchers (mostly) honest and fuels innovation, but it holds back social change. I say mostly because corporate interests fund a fair amount of research – the bias in data. In the words of the National Institutes of Health, "industry-sponsored studies tend to be biased in favor of the sponsor's products."[209] Researchers are increasingly dependent on industry sponsorship as government funding for research drops. (I suspect corporate lobbying is at play.) A Yale School of Medicine study found that industry funding for research rose from 32% to 62% from 1980 to 2000.[210] The *British Medical Journal* found that 68% of industry-run trials are published within one year, as opposed to 11% of academic-run trials.[211] Fossil fuel companies gave $700 million to 27 United States universities over 10 years for climate research. Call me cynical, but I expect they wanted a return on their investment.[212] Perversely, the drowning prevention field could exploit their lack of funding by lauding the fact that research studies in their field have integrity since they are not impacted by big money.

The reality remains that researchers need funding. Standards for research are high and subject to scrutiny for a reason. Bad research is worse than no research, and unethical and sloppy research can cause real harm if it is adopted. Corporations and competitors to change benefit substantially from slowing or hiding dissenting research from the public and policymakers. There must be a better way, a more balanced way. As a starting point, I would like all research to include a widely available, open source, plain language summary of the issue (no more than eighth-grade reading level), the outcome of the research, recommended behavioral changes, how to measure change, and the limitations of the research (last, not first), presented as bullet points and with a link to the full paper. I am also opposed to most research languishing behind paywalls, away from those who need to access the research to implement successful programs. The cost of paywalls serves as another untenable financial barrier to change for small organizations with a strong resistance to changing the system. (Follow the money.)

There is a chasm between the "beyond reasonable doubt" cautious researcher approach and the "swing for the fences" corporate approach that can be narrowed without damaging the integrity of research. We already have research which shows that teaching survival swimming skills reduces the chance of drowning by 93%, and regular swimming lessons reduce the chance of drowning by 88%.[213] Compelling numbers support the importance of learning to swim. It should be enough. Imagine if all research was subject to the well-marketed attitude of, "Well, we really need more proof ... If there was just more evidence ... There are flaws in the research ..." because, with lasting behavioral change, there are far more contributing variables that are difficult, if not impossible, to separate and quantify monetarily, much less to ensure consistency and give the numbers validity.

To point out the absurdity of refusing to change behavior without absolute certainty, consider the difficulties in financially justifying the teaching of survival swimming to an 8-year-old:

Track each child for the rest of their life to prove they did not drown as a result of swimming lessons.

Identify each instance where survival swim skills were used and each instance where knowledge of water safety allowed the child to avoid a dangerous situation, to save the life of another person, or to teach the skills to another person.

Perform a cost–benefit analysis by calculating the value of the child's life and the probability of early death or brain damage against the average cost of survival swim programs.

Make allowances for the location of the lessons (portable pool, permanent pool, or open water), the number of children in each class, the qualifications of the instructor, the cost of the lessons, the cost relative to other expenses or investments in health and welfare, the mental and physical skills of the children, and their typical surroundings.

Evaluate and quantify parental and family support and cultural mores around learning to swim.

Monitor and measure exposure to media and education campaigns and measure the impact on attitudes and behaviors.

The high number of independent variables and the cost of tracking a large enough group to make the results statistically significant would be extremely costly, logistically impossible, and would take so many years that by the time the program is proven to be effective and cost-effective, developments in survival swimming and water safety may have changed, nullifying the impact of the results. Never mind the clear ethical concerns of having control groups of children who did not learn to swim or were put in danger by tossing them into the water and watching to see if they drowned. By the time the study is complete, thousands of children may have drowned because they did not receive swimming instruction as they awaited quantifiable justification for the lessons with 98% certainty.

I am not in favor of weakened research standards. In fact, the opposite; we need stronger standards of financial disclosure and publication of research. Sources of research funding should be disclosed. The financial interests of funders should be disclosed. Bias related to financial gain should be disclosed. Research summaries should be widely available and mechanisms provided to make studies available for organizations that cannot afford access.

We enter uncharted territory as we start to shift focus, so expect doubt, criticism, conflict, and botched attempts, but we have to start somewhere. Changing the way organizations and the public perceive the value of social change will take time and concerted effort. The intent of this book is to argue for that change in mindset and to suggest a starting point, but measurable change will only occur if many people and organizations begin to consistently challenge the status quo while developing consistent new protocols for measuring value and success. Individual organizations hurling themselves at the barricades won't work as effectively as everyone putting their shoulder to the barricade and pushing at the same time.

Break down all the variables and potential outcomes into measurable pieces. Begin with two categories – the cost of changing and the cost of not changing. The cost of changing quantifies how much it will cost to change a behavior and the value of that behavior change. The cost of not changing quantifies what it would cost society if the behavior is not changed. Aim to market the behavior change that also avoids financial risk for government and corporations. Most organizations stop at the most basic level – the cost of existing programs and budgets – not at the cost of not changing. We are stuck in defense mode instead of marketing the benefits. Because budgets in the social change field are dwarfed by budgets in the for-profit field, focusing on existing program costs reinforces the comparatively low value of change. Developing a wider and more accurate assessment of the costs and benefits of change requires a more creative approach. It involves maximizing economies of scale, explaining both cost and value, quantifying partnerships and strategic alliances, and assigning value to outcomes.

Economies of scale means that the more you produce, the less it costs. The goal is for each organization to function at the most efficient level to attain optimal economies of scale. If you are teaching survival swimming, a permanent or portable pool is a big expense. At maximum capacity, you can teach 4,000 children per year in that pool, but you currently have the funding to teach only 1,000 children. This means that the cost of using the pool is spread across 1,000 children instead of 4,000 children, which increases fourfold the cost of teaching each child. If you can reach your optimal economy of scale (teaching 4,000 children in one pool every year), the cost of teaching each child is very low, typically ranging from $4 to $45 per child, depending on the program and location. (Note: in Bangladesh they use bamboo poles to create enclosed lesson areas in open water.) Be conscious of diseconomies of scale or the point where the cost begins to increase again. In our example, teaching 5,000 children would require investing in a second pool. Bigger isn't always better. Optimize your resources.

Once you know your optimal level of operating, communicate the cost and the value. The cost is the actual money spent. The value is relative to every other program or experience where the money could be spent. Communicate in clear, easy-to-understand language and market the information to your target audience – the people whose behavior you want to change. Save the Children tells you that the cost of $1 a day provides one child with basic education, health, nutrition and developmental help, but the value of that investment is buried in their website.[214] Heifer International tells you that the cost to buy a flock of chickens is $20.[215] The value is creating a sustainable small business for a family to support themselves by selling the eggs, although they rely more on nonspecific "change a life" messages, which means different things to different people. There would be a greater impact on attitudes and behaviors if they were to specify how lives are changed in terms the donors would understand. What does a chicken mean in terms of income, education, and healthcare? When you don't state both the cost *and* the value, and correlate the cost with the value, the impact is lessened. Tell your audience what they are buying. There is a reason why for-profits market the value of their product or service, but don't advertise executive salaries, stock buybacks, and shareholder returns.

Value for many programs can be hard to explain. Look for comparisons that can be easily understood. For survival swimming, we know that the drowning rates for children who complete the SwimSafe program in Bangladesh are 93% lower than their peers. We also know that there is herd immunity, meaning that even if a child did not take the class, their risk of drowning is lower because their trained peers are more likely to be able to rescue them or keep them from getting into danger in the first place. The value of survival swimming is not understood if the risk of drowning is not understood. A more commonly understood concept is that when healthy children are vaccinated against disease, they are protected from the disease. Herd immunity means that a child with a compromised immune system who could not be vaccinated is less likely to contract a disease if their peers are vaccinated. If we apply the concept of vaccination to the less understood area of water safety, then teaching water safety and survival swimming acts as a "vaccination" against drowning and protects children who cannot learn to swim because most children are learning how to rescue others without endangering themselves.

Don't limit quantifying cost and value to your program. Extend evaluation of the reduced costs and increased value associated with your strategic partnerships too. Although collaboration is the flavor of the day in the social change field, the attitude remains that collaboration is dividing up a small funding pie, not working to create a larger pie. It is like asking a 2-year-old to give half their cookie to a younger sibling with no bonus cookie in sight. For-profit companies do not spend all their energy fighting over a tiny piece of the market; they focus their energy on expanding their market, both internally and through strategic partnerships. Porsche attracted a new customer base by introducing an SUV and sedan into their lineup.[216] McDonald's introduced "healthy" options to their menu to cash in on the wellness trend.[217] Sports clothing manufacturers collaborate with professional athletes to call attention to both the clothing and the athletes. Eddie Bauer and Ford collaborated to bring outdoor style to cars and trucks.[218] These companies grow by leveraging each other's strengths. They don't form partnerships to be nice or to give away their assets; they base them on intentional strategies for growth and increased value for both parties.

Broaden your horizon when you look for strategic partnerships but maintain the same discipline of quantifying cost and value. Bundling refers to selling different items together for cost-efficiency or customer ease. It is the reason why computers come preloaded with operating software and your car has a sound system or sunroof. The bundling of goods and services makes good business sense and often includes creating partnerships in totally different business areas. We take it for granted that children learn math, science, reading, and geography at one school. Imagine if they had to attend different schools for each subject. The costs would increase and the perceived value would decrease. Bundling services together increases both the perceived and real value and decreases costs.

The easiest way to bundle services is to go directly to your audience and offer the full menu; don't wait for them to come to you. If a person goes to a domestic violence shelter or is rescued from a human trafficking situation, the urgent need is protection. Once the immediate need is addressed, other services can be bundled through partnerships: legal aid, job training, parenting classes, tutoring for children, medical services, counseling, assistance in relocating, clothing, money management tutorials, and aid in repairing or establishing a credit history.

To create the right bundle of services, think through the problem using the five whys and W's. A large market for African animal trophies and horns exists outside of the continent. Poaching occurs because there is an external demand, a lack of alternative internal employment, and a lack of understanding about the importance of animals to both the ecosystem and the economic security of local communities. There is also a lack of understanding that African resources, including the animals, are being exploited by non-African forces. The all-female Black Mamba Anti-Poaching Unit has a primary goal of identifying poachers in South Africa, but they are bundling their attack on poaching with teaching children about the importance of protecting the wildlife.[219] Understanding that poaching is a source of income in an area where there is high unemployment, they also focus on providing alternative economic opportunities in the region. This occurs, in part, by creating active rhino conservation areas, which draw attention to the issue and attract tourists who pay to see live animals, bringing revenue to local economies. Such bundling initiatives leverage local knowledge and talent while also addressing underlying issues like employment, and consequently have a greater chance of success than outsiders dictating that "poaching is bad." Positive reinforcement over shame and blame.

Broaden your vision when identifying the competition. Out-of-control fires regularly destroy millions of acres of forest and open land, causing economic losses, health issues, significant climate problems, and represent a serious risk to a number of endangered species.[220] Separating economic and policy solutions spearheaded by national and local governments from social and cultural grassroots activists leads to a fragmented approach, which can easily be dismantled by the competition. Fires have an impact on a wide range of issues, in terms of both cost and value. Harness a broad swath of stakeholders with a coherent strategy and crush the opposition.

The calculations needed to assign values to outcomes are not simple. They must be accurate and defensible, which means enlisting experts in finance, statistics, and economics. Be prepared to change or discontinue programs that do not pass the cost–benefit test, no matter how much you love them. We cannot afford to compete only on emotion. Gut feelings must be backed up by solid indicators of success. For-profit businesses that don't get real results don't survive, and neither should social change programs.

It can be hard to acknowledge that something isn't working. Failure, and learning from that failure, is a strong indicator of future success.[221] It isn't the failure directly, it is the ability to look critically at what has and has not worked and to have the resilience and determination to try again. As Thomas Edison said, "I have gotten lots of results! I know several thousand things that won't work."[222] Edison has been marketed primarily as an inventor, but he was one of the most prominent businessmen in the United States during his lifetime, attracting investors like J. P. Morgan and the Vanderbilt family.[223] He said, "Anything that won't sell, I don't want to invent. Its sale is proof of utility, and utility is success."[224] Inventions don't see the light of day without inventors being willing to acknowledge what is failing and demonstrate effectiveness and financial viability. Neither does social change.

When weak or ineffective programs die, it frees up resources and talent for better programs, but sometimes good programs are intentionally killed by the activists themselves. To identify your most dangerous competition, see who benefits financially by maintaining the status quo. Eliminate or alter the competition by providing better monetary outcomes and perceived value. Identify who will suffer financially from the desired behavior change and assess their financial stake. Is it one small segment of this competitor's business that needs to change, or is it their entire business model? One small segment might be open to negotiation and finding an alternative model. Destroying the business entirely requires a different approach. To identify all your competitors, once again ask the five whys and W's until you have a clear map. Know your competition. The old adages, "know your enemies" and "keep your friends close and your enemies closer" have been around for a long time for good reason – they are usually true.

Any organization that is generating a profit is successfully changing behavior. Don't get stuck on the idea that behavior change must be positive. Think of the sugar and fossil fuel industries.[225] If profit is a positive dollar amount on the bottom line of an income statement, it doesn't matter if outcomes are measured positively with lives saved, disease reduced, or children taught to swim, or if outcomes are measured negatively with more drug addicts or more rhinos killed. Profit is a measurement of successful behavior change.

Contacts are a way of directing behavioral change. Development of the COVID-19 vaccine is exhibit A. The United States government alone spent more than $30 billion on vaccines, paying for development, guaranteeing a market, and ensuring the vaccines would be provided free of charge to the public, thereby creating strong demand.[226] As of March 2021, 98.12% of vaccine development came from public funding.[227] As soon as the federal government stopped paying for the vaccines, pharmaceutical firms increased the price by 56%–73%, with more increases expected and no need to repay R&D costs.[228] Taxpayer money paid for development and distribution, but shareholders and executives benefitted from the lack of negotiations, repeating the pattern of the 2008 financial bailout. It is important to negotiate contracts with a long-term perspective, even in a crisis.

It doesn't have to be a complex global problem to use these techniques and get results. Say you want to start a small community garden with an apiary for attracting honey bees because you are concerned that global honey bee populations are rapidly reducing for unknown reasons.[229] You have found a small piece of land but lack funding and broad community support. Identify the competition. Who wants to use the land for another purpose? People in the community may not know that honey bee pollination is responsible for an estimated one-third of the world's food supply, but their populations are collapsing.[230] Some simply dislike bees or are afraid of being stung. Larger issues, like attitudes about climate breakdown, may influence people's opinions. If they don't believe a climate breakdown is occurring, affecting the global environment and many species, they may be less likely to believe that individual species are threatened. The idea of a community garden may also be of concern. Who deserves to benefit? What sort of people will work in the garden? Who will be allowed to harvest the produce? Is there a danger in working near bees?

In this situation, the primary competition is lack of awareness and incorrect information. Having identified the competition, identify collaborators. Think about who benefits from a community garden and apiary. Local restaurants could tap into the movement towards locally sourced food by serving produce and honey from the garden. Local coffee shops benefit by serving local honey, showing they are giving back to the community that sustains their business. Schools could incorporate field trips to the garden and apiary into their science, health, and social studies curriculums. Local gardeners could benefit from an increase in pollinators. Local garden centers could benefit with the improved pollination and increased understanding of the importance of plants that attract bees, resulting in more plant sales. Vacant land will be put to good use, eliminating time and expense by the village and reducing the dangers that come with overgrown or neglected properties. Excess produce could potentially be used to help local food pantries or churches to feed the hungry. Gardening can ease stress, keep you limber, and improve mental health, all outcomes that local hospitals and medical groups promote through their wellness campaigns.[231] A community garden not only helps those who work in the garden, but also encourages other residents to garden and reap the same benefits.

Once you have identified your competition and collaborators, begin to calculate the financial value of the change. If produce and honey can be sold to local restaurants and coffee shops, the revenue can be used to sustain the garden or go towards other clearly identified projects in the community. Local garden centers could be approached to donate a percentage of sales directly to the project, a "bee garden week promotion." In return, the village would widely advertise their involvement and encourage residents to purchase their plants from these supporters. Preemptively counteract the nay-sayers who protest that money for plants is wasted by reaching out to influential people in the community to support the garden and the planting. Market hard-dollar, easily quantifiable efforts:

landscaping, trees, and plants all improve property values and the desirability of a community, which makes it easier to sell property at a higher value.[232] Reinforce the message by applying for recognition through national organizations. Use newsletters, local newspapers, and community forums to educate the public about the importance of bees and the native plants they pollinate. Enlist avid local gardeners to write a column or give a seminar at the local library on the best bee-friendly plants. Use all the financial arguments to demonstrate that no action or alternative use of the land passes the cost–benefit test.

Support alternative behaviors. Cities that have been successful in introducing bicycles to reduce auto traffic and reduce carbon emissions have not done so simply by banning autos or putting out bicycles and hoping for the best. Over 500 cities have successful bicycle-sharing schemes because they identified the competition, communicated the need for the change, made it easy to change, made it socially desirable to change, and supported the change.[233] The competition overcame the cost arguments (cheaper than buying a bicycle, no maintenance charges, and competitive rental pricing that makes it far cheaper than driving or using public transportation); ease of use (available for rent in a wide number of places and the ability to drop-off in a different place); convenience (changes to traffic patterns and increasing the number of bike lanes); and public perception (easily identifiable bicycles backed by an aggressive public relations campaign).[234] Not every city has been immediately successful. Just because change occurs positively in one city does not mean it can be quickly or simply implemented in another without marketing the behavior change to each population in a way that addresses local concerns.[235] Adaptation and evolution are key to success.

Balance emotion and facts. The 2014 Climate Summit opening ceremony at the United Nations featured a poem presented by Kathy Jetnil-Kijiner of the Marshall Islands, which evocatively demonstrated the impact of climate change on her family.[236] Emotions put the data in context for the discussion and subsequent recommendations. To engage your audience, create and communicate solid data and financial arguments in a way that also engages emotion, with emotion in a supportive role, not as the dominant "pull at the heartstrings" or "inspire guilt" roles that have been the common default. Emotions do not create substantial and sustainable streams of revenue. To be successful, convince your audience of both the worth of your mission, using emotion, and measurable, cost-effective, and sustainable actions, backed by research and data.

Selling products can create an emotional tie to potential donors and the public, or not. Too often, a good idea is simply copied without thinking through the desired behavior change. The first ribbon was a yellow ribbon in support of the Iran hostages in 1979.[237] The red AIDS ribbon followed, then the pink breast cancer ribbon, and now there is a rainbow of ribbons for every imaginable cause, which has lessened the impact. The first idea is brilliant, the 37th rendition is boring. Cause bracelets followed the ribbon trend. Some research shows that people who buy charity bracelets are more interested in following a fashion trend and are less interested in the cause than people who don't buy the bracelets.[238]

Avoid products and symbols that make you a follower, not a leader. Invest your time and money in creating symbols that clearly differentiate your cause or organization. Over time, just seeing the symbol will evoke the right emotions and actions if you are marketing your cause and organization effectively. Smokey Bear for preventing forest fires.[239] The World Wide Fund for Nature panda for wildlife conservation.[240] There is a reason that companies invest in logos that the public instantly associate with their company and brand. Logos and symbols evoke emotion and help to build a relationship, which then allows the company to market behavior change. McDonald's golden arches. The Nike swoosh. Apple's apple.[241] Before you sell products designed to increase engagement and generate revenue, make sure they are under a visual umbrella that is recognizable and evokes the right emotions. Brand consistency works.

Komen excel at generating substantial revenue through their three-day walks and Race for the Cure fundraising events. These events serve the dual purpose of engaging their audience and creating revenue.[242] The autism awareness campaign Light It Up Blue engages corporations, governments, well-known monuments, and individuals to light their buildings blue on a designated day. They also encourage organizations to donate 20% of their net profits to the founding organization in return for use of the logo (intellectual property), which also allows them to retain control over the campaign.[243] Toys for Tots.[244] The World's Largest Swimming Lesson.[245] Your school mascot. These are all examples of brand-name events that raise both funds and awareness. The events don't have to be as large or well known to be successful. Small community events can mobilize, engage, and become an important way of strengthening community ties, like the annual Daisy Dash 5k race, which raises funds for local charities and schools in a small town.[246] When a wealthy resident accidentally planted daisy seeds instead of grass seed, the daisy fields became a unifying visual symbol. Participating in the race has become a family tradition for many and a symbol of community solidarity.

Extend linking emotion and money by being creative in how you attract and compensate the best talent. Workers in all fields have varying perceptions of appropriate rewards.[247] Rewards can be measured in a number of ways. Nonmonetary rewards are valued by employees (providing their monetary compensation is fair to start with).[248] To quantify the value of nonmonetary rewards, simply ask people what they value through surveys or a menu of benefit options. When I was in my twenties, I worked as a manager for a consulting firm. One of the perks of the job was a company car. The only problem was that I didn't value a company car. I already had a car. I wouldn't have been able to see over the steering wheel of the proposed behemoth of a company car. I didn't like driving automatic transmission cars. I would have had to find parking in my crowded urban neighborhood and pay taxes on the price of the car. I rode public transport to work, and all my clients were an airplane ride away, so I wouldn't even use the company car for work. I asked if I could transfer the value of the car to additional vacation time so I could travel, something that was important to me. There was no understanding that I valued time more than the proposed reward and the company wouldn't adapt, so I lost compensation. Understand what motivates the people you want to hire. Each generation brings different values to the workplace.[249] Don't create a customized plan for every person you hire, but understand that if you are going to benefit from true diversity in an organization, the most cost-effective way of providing value is to look at how you can provide the best employees with better actual and perceived value.

Social change causes have an enormous competitive advantage over most traditional businesses because they intrinsically provide an experience that most people value – a purpose.[250] Exploit that competitive advantage. If you begin to level the playing field by paying competitively and providing a purpose that has both real and perceived value, you begin to crush the competition, taking the best employees and weakening organizations that are promoting damaging behaviors. Provide direction. Make the right tools available. Inspire people. And then let them loose to create a social movement.

Chapter 8 Worksheet

1. Look at your budget. What are the percentages by category? What does your budget tell you about your priorities?
2. What language do you use to describe your goals, programs, and achievements? How do you quantify them? What financial value do you apply?
3. List the top-paid people in your organization. What are their skill sets? What does this tell you about your priorities?
4. What data is available that can communicate your goals and programs in monetary terms? What data is missing? Can the impact be communicated in monetary terms?
5. Look at your programs. What opportunities exist for bundling services with other organizations? How can you measure and communicate the cost-effectiveness of bundling services?
6. How do you measure behavior change? Can the impact of the change be measured financially?
7. Who, or what companies, are profiting financially from existing behaviors? What is the specific behavior they are supporting? How is this behavior competition to your goals? Name your competitors.
8. To change behaviors, is it necessary to eliminate, weaken, or collaborate with the competition? Brainstorm ways of marketing the necessity to your supporters.
9. What are the financial benefits of changing behavior for your target audience? How can you market those benefits?
10. What success stories about behavior change can you tell your audience? List five ways you can interact with your audience.

Chapter 9

MOBILIZE THE TROOPS

Creating social change takes more than the efforts of one group. A number of independent parts and different approaches are needed, but a system failure in one area weakens an entire cause. Imagine if a group of soldiers decided that attacking a target was a good idea and headed off on their own, with no discussion on how the target fits into the big picture. No specialized training. No tactical support. No supply chain. No check to ensure their equipment or weaponry is appropriate. No communications with other soldiers in the area. No plan B if plan A doesn't work. No "what happens next?" plan. Such a venture is not only likely to fail, but could potentially undermine an entire mission – harming innocents, endangering other soldiers, extending or expanding the conflict, and damaging diplomatic relations. There is a reason why the military does not tolerate such individual whims. The same holds true on a broader scale. Imagine if the Air Force didn't bother to confirm plans with the Army and the Navy. Or the Marines decided they had a better idea, but the Coast Guard didn't agree and sabotaged their plan. Loose cannons miss the mark when faced with a more organized force.

A successful cause requires a coordinated team that builds and supports a social movement. Each group works towards a common goal but with different tasks, different skills, and different materials – all coordinated to ensure the best outcome.

By applying the techniques in the earlier chapters of this book, you are almost ready to launch the social movement for your cause. You are clear on your specific mission and how it fits into the larger cause. You have leveraged the data and research to understand the behavior change that is necessary. You have created data-driven and financial arguments for change. You have identified the competition and developed a plan to reduce or eliminate them. You know your audience, you have diversified your core team, and you have developed a network of strategic partners both within your immediate area of interest and those that are supportive or are also affected. You understand the broader social and cultural context for the behavior and have grouped your strategic partners by emotion, research, and action.

Now, it is time to lock in the change, and communication is the key. Communication is defined as "a process by which information is exchanged between individuals through a common system of symbols, signs, or behavior."[252] For communication to be effective, both the sender and the receiver need to interpret the message in the same way. If you ask for an apple, I shouldn't hand you an orange. Transmitting information implies a one-way flow of information. When communication is flowing only one way, it is easy to become complacent and overconfident because you never hear dissent or disagreement. One-way communication is cheap and easy. You state your position, launch your campaign, trumpet through your chosen media channels, and assume your audience will simply follow your directions. However, if you have ever had a human relationship, you know that expecting the other person to blindly follow new directions rarely happens. Relying on one-way communication also hands a major advantage to the competition, who will leap in to divert the conversation. To lock in the change, make communication a two-way street. Break down the process into two parts: how the message is developed and how the message is communicated. To be effective, test whether your words and images are interpreted as intended and adopted by your audience on a consistent basis. Messages should be positive, simple, consistent, and repetitive.

- **Positive**. There is a large body of research showing that people are far more likely to internalize the desired behavior if they are positively motivated. To change behavior, make people feel good about the change. Messages of doom and gloom only engage fear and shame, emotions we try to avoid long term. Trying to convince people that they want to give up something that brings them joy doesn't work; it is the cod liver oil in the unheated shack instead of the champagne and caviar on the yacht in the Mediterranean.

- **Simple**. The most people can reliably remember is seven things, give or take two things.[253] It is the reason Bell Labs made phone numbers seven digits long, but seven can still be overwhelming when presenting messages designed to change behavior.[254] To deliver memorable messages, aim for no more than three main points.[255] Stop, drop and roll. Don't drink and drive. Always swim with others. Simple, concise, and directive messages that fit within the current average attention span of eight seconds.[256]

Tell people what to do simply. Don't ask, don't reason, and don't supply all the explanations behind the action. A common concern is that each cause is so complex that we cannot possibly boil it down to sound bites, so we try to elaborate on the message, often at length and in excruciating detail. All issues are complex, but you cannot deliver the full message unless you have your audience's attention. This is best achieved by using positive, simple, consistent, and repetitive messages.

- **Consistent**. Virtually every adult in every country understands that a red light or a red octagonal sign means stop.[257] The message (stop) and the visual symbol (red light or octagonal sign) have infiltrated the public's consciousness and consistently result in the desired behavior, which improves safety and decreases injury and mortality rates. Imagine if a rainbow of lights was used, or the shape of the sign was sometimes a square, sometimes a triangle, or sometimes an octagon. Chaos, death, and injury would ensue. Communicate the main message positively, simply, and consistently. Adjust the supporting messages for different audiences and across different media, communicating additional information where necessary, but the starting point should always be the same.

- **Repetitive**. We don't say, "Look both ways before you cross the street" once to a child and hope the lesson sinks in. We do it thousands of times, using the exact same words, until we see the desired behavior consistently and without prompting, so we know it has been internalized. The same repetition that we instinctually use with children to reinforce key messages is effective when communicating positive, simple, and consistent messages repetitively.

Sometimes a primary message is communicated at too high a level. The message is about calculus while your audience is still working on addition and subtraction. Most people haven't learned about correct behavior simply because they haven't been taught, and they don't understand why they should bother to learn. Explain the change in simple language. Bring your audience to the point where they are ready to hear your message. Start your campaign with the most basic level of information and build on the information over time. Don't assume your audience's starting point of knowledge. Ask questions to identify their starting point.

To embed the primary message in people's minds and behaviors, supply a range of supporting information that elaborates on the primary behavior, explains the reason for the behavior, outlines the negative outcomes if the behavior is not followed, and reinforces the correct behavior. The primary message does not change – STOP, don't drink and drive, always swim near a lifeguard – but the way you communicate the details to your distinctive audiences should be different. If you are addressing drunk driving, your target audience includes parents, adolescents, schools, law enforcement, and owners of establishments that sell liquor. Adolescents react differently to risk than adults because their brains are changing rapidly.[258] Adults hear the messages differently when they are reacting as parents concerned about their children versus when they are the ones out socializing and consuming alcohol. Tying all the supporting messages together under one descriptive action-oriented message creates a higher probability that the behavior will become internalized and sustainable over time and across multiple scenarios.

Say it with me again: Positive. Simple. Consistent. Repetitive.

You have done your market analysis. You know the issue. You have core messages that are positive, simple, consistent, and repetitive. You have supporting messages tailored to each of your audiences. Now it is time to deliver the messages. To be successful, deliver layers of messages in a range of mediums through a network of influencers and audiences.

It is far easier to reach a wide audience by finding the person or people who have the most influence with your audience and have them communicate the message. The basic premise is that you don't have to convince everyone, you just need to convince the right people. Don't confuse power or wealth with influence. Power and wealth are often traits of people with influence, but not always. Power is also unsurprisingly linked with men, but influencers cast a wider and more diverse net."[259] It was Malala Yousafzai, an 18-year-old student from Pakistan, whose influence helped convince the United Nations to extend the goal of education from nine years to twelve years for all children as part of the seventeen Sustainable Development Goals.[260] Candy Lightner transformed America's view of drunk driving, founded MADD (Mothers Against Drunk Driving), and fought for stricter laws after her 13-year-old daughter was killed by a repeat driving-under-the-influence offender.[261] Lilly Ledbetter sued Goodyear for equal pay for women, ultimately sending the issue to the Supreme Court before being signed into law.[262] Nadina Riggsbee has been instrumental in changing policy, promoting legislation, and changing building codes after her two children drowned.[263] Look for true influencers in your field, those who actually make a difference, not just those who give speeches or write checks.

The more visible and obvious influencers include professional athletes, musicians, and Hollywood stars – high-profile individuals who have realized that they can use their influence with the public to raise the profile of any number of causes, from genocide to refugees to AIDS to mental illness. Not On Our Watch was founded by a group of men with enormous cultural influence – Don Cheadle, George Clooney, Matt Damon, Brad Pitt, David

Pressman, and Jerry Weintraub. Dedicated to drawing upon the voices of cultural leaders to protect and assist the vulnerable, marginalized, and displaced, they merged with The Sentry in 2019, collaborating for greater impact "to disable multinational predatory networks that benefit from violent conflict, repression, and kleptocracy."[264] UNICEF has enlisted an impressive roster of celebrity ambassadors who have proved tireless in "mobilizing the support necessary to improve the lives of children and ensure their basic human rights."[265] Heads Together is a mental health initiative spearheaded by the Prince and Princess of Wales to tackle stigma around mental health.[266] The overlooked field of drowning prevention has benefitted from the attention of HSH Princess Charlene of Monaco with the establishment of her Princess Charlene of Monaco Foundation, benefitting 1.79 million people in 604 projects across 44 countries.[267]

Influencers with the ability to attract media attention or to be invited to address governments or the United Nations are never enough. The greatest power comes from leveraging both top-down and bottom-up influence to create a powerful pincer move for change. Postmenopausal women have proven to be powerful activists – ordinary women who are, in their words, old enough that they have nothing to lose and a determination to protect the world's children. Paola Gianturco's book *Grandmother Power: A Global Phenomenon* profiles grandmothers who have become fearless and potent activists.[268] Imagine if the men at Not On Our Watch were to partner with the grandmothers in communities in Darfur, Sudan, Burma, and Zimbabwe. Their effectiveness could be increased ten-fold. Ordinary people who have influence in their communities are at least as powerful as, and often more powerful than, high-level or outside influencers. I met Viraj from Mauritius and Moses from Uganda at a drowning prevention conference where they compared notes on lifesaving in resource-poor environments. Both men have influence in their individual communities, but that individual influence was strengthened by working together and adapting approaches to their environments.[269]

Connectors have an influence indirectly but powerfully. Connectors can see the big picture and think strategically to identify the necessary resources. A connector can take an outwardly passive role, such as brokering introductions and letting the parties decide how to progress, or take a more active role by developing a strategic plan, identifying all the necessary people and resources, and putting it all together. Connectors can match people to roles, money to causes, or organizations to projects. Connectors can focus on a relatively small community or have a global reach. A true connector will find that the skills come naturally and will measure success by the outcome, not by their individual contribution. Their influence comes from being able to put the right people together, to make the sum more powerful than the individual parts. "Connector" is not a job title, and you won't find many true connectors working for only one organization. Their power and their enjoyment of the process comes from casting a wider net to form connections that result in change.

It is simple to say that networks, influencers, and connectors are important, but they are difficult to leverage at full capacity. Whether it is a small community venture or a global initiative, taking the time to build the infrastructure for communication is as important as building roads and railways to transport goods and people. You can make the best widgets in the world, but if you cannot get them to your audience, they are worthless. Leveraging the strengths of multiple groups of influencers using a three-pronged approach increases your chance of success. Break down the desired behavior change into three categories: emotion, research, and action.

- **Emotion.** Those who have experienced a loss or injury, especially parents who have lost a child, bring real-life experience to the data about the speed and ease with which drowning can occur and can relate emotionally to other parents in a valuable and highly effective manner. They have the ability to harness emotions and connect with others in a deeply personal and persuasive manner. They supply the stories, both positive and negative. The Achilles' heel of this group is that they can have difficulty separating from the emotion and can focus on the solution that would have prevented their individual loss rather than improving the broader picture. This is especially problematic if data shows the cause of death was not typical.

- **Research**. Researchers provide solutions that can be implemented, including the data to support the need for interventions and to measure their effectiveness. The Achilles' heel of this group is the lack of translation from theory into practice. Information often languishes behind firewalls or in the hallowed halls of academia and conferences rather than being marketed and made available to directly influence program development and evaluation. How research is used in real life should be as important a metric for advancement as the number of papers published. Research, data, and analysis need to be marketed effectively, using emotion to make them relevant to the public, along with clear action steps for people to follow regarding communication and implementation.

- **Action**. The action prong demonstrates appropriate behavior and intervenes when there is danger. This leg is important for teaching, demonstrating, and reinforcing the correct behaviors identified through research and encouraged through emotion. The action group may contain either top-down or bottom-up influencers, but don't make the mistake of confusing action with influence – something that is easy to do when dealing with an action group. The Achilles' heel of this group is being too action oriented. They instinctually leap forward to action without taking the time to assess and evoke the right emotions or without integrating current research or measuring outcomes.

Leveraging all three approaches simultaneously allows you to identify and test the ideal behaviors, create an emotional argument for adopting the behaviors, and provide the training, education, and role models to learn and maintain the behaviors. Emotion, research, and action on their own won't change behavior, but when combined they are a powerful tool.

Academic papers, meetings, and conferences all require a significant amount of expertise, time, planning, and money, and they have smaller and more exclusive audiences. That level of expertise and homogeneous audience can be a liability. Just as it is easy to be one step removed from face-to-face contact with media or paper communications and assume the message is being received and appreciated, so small groups provide an easy way for everyone to feel good because they are receiving recognition from their peers. No idea truly prospers when exposed only in the rarified air of meetings, conferences, and academic journals. The best ideas and programs need the bacteria, dirt, and scrutiny of the real world to thrive and expand.

These smaller self-selected groups – whether they are a meeting of two people, a conference of one thousand people, or the readers of academic journals – serve an important purpose by introducing ideas, inviting constructive criticism, weeding out poorly contrived or executed studies, and moving people to consensus on complex issues. Where they fail is their inability to translate and communicate the results to a wider audience. Ideas and programs should not languish within the confines of these small groups. Commit to translating your results to the wider public in simple, consistent language and through a range of channels. Get outside the paywalls.

The success in virtually eradicating guinea worm disease demonstrates how low-technology behavior change translates theory into action in the real world. Since 1986, the Carter Center has led the international campaign to eradicate guinea worm disease, working closely with ministries of health and local communities, the U.S. Centers for Disease Control and Prevention, the World Health Organization, UNICEF, and other partners. By translating expertise and theory into community-wide efforts to change behavior, guinea worm disease is set to become the second human disease in history to be eradicated, after smallpox. It will be the first disease to be eliminated without the use of a vaccine or medicine.[270]

Share information within your network. Newsletters, email blasts, social media posts, meetings, and conferences can all be effective ways of building a community and sharing information, but they can also lead to a false sense of security. If you send 1,000 newsletters every month but the same 10 people are donating and showing up for events, the newsletter is not having the desired effect. The same goes for email blasts and all forms of social media.

"Shared" or "liked" may not link to action. The more effort you put into something, the harder it can be to accept that nothing is changing. As the old adage goes, insanity is doing the same thing over and over again and expecting different results. The problem isn't with those receiving the message; the problem is with the message. Conduct a focus group or online survey to find out what your audience needs and expects. Relentlessly and ruthlessly track what content is engaging them. Take the extra step to make sure the message matches the audience. A few years ago, the media was covering what they incorrectly called "secondary" or "dry drowning." Professionals in the water safety field wanted to react with the correct technical information and terminology. Their focus was on the correct *words*, not the correct *action*. Meanwhile, parents were panicking about how to protect their children, not the definition. Discussions raged behind the scenes about what needed to be communicated rather than understanding what information the target audience wanted to know. (Note: Drowning only comes in two types – fatal and nonfatal. There is no such thing as secondary or dry drowning; however, parents want to know how to keep their child safe and what words to use to express their concern to medical professionals to get the appropriate care, since even medical professionals don't always know the signs of nonfatal drowning.[271])

Look for ways to embed your message into all forms of media, in the same way that the concept of designated drivers was successfully embedded into American consciousness using top-rated television programs, public service announcements, public relations campaigns, and the support of politicians, federal agencies, advocacy groups, sports leagues, major corporations, police departments, and brewers and distillers. These efforts, combined with new laws and stricter enforcement, resulted in a 24% reduction in traffic fatalities in four years and paved the way for antidrug messages to be embedded in popular media.[272]

As technology continues to evolve and infiltrate our lives, social media will be used more aggressively to spread messages designed to change behavior. Launched in 2004, today Facebook has over three billion users, doubling since 2016.[273] Instagram attracted 2.4 billion users in a short time, eclipsing Twitter's (now X) 421 million users.[274] YouTube has over 2.7 billion unique visits each month, watching over one billion hours of videos every day.[275] Developing and executing an effective social media strategy is confounding to many organizations, as social media is really meant for individuals. There can be a backlash if you are perceived as invading people's personal space or pushing a corporate agenda.

Identify your audience. Look at the demographics and the level of engagement on your existing social media platforms, including your website. Set baseline measurements to track your progress, review your analytics weekly, and pay attention to what has the most shares, views, and comments. It will teach you about what interests your audience and can save you a lot of time and money when you develop larger communication campaigns. Think of social media as market research. Be intentional and consistent about your brand. Match your audiences with the best social media platforms. Be clear on what you want to accomplish. Be brutal in culling topics or approaches that don't engage.

Engage! The biggest mistake made in social media is pushing information. No one wants to be lectured. My favorite safety video is "Dumb Ways to Die."[276] The Australian sponsor is promoting train safety, but over 275 million people have learned about several ways that potentially fatal accidents can occur. Kids and teens love the video, so they watch. They love it so much that it has spawned apps, interactive games, and a store. You really don't want your friends thinking "that was a dumb way to die" (yes, a teen would think that). It is an amazing use of leveraging age-appropriate humor with a stick-in-your-head tune. Virgin America's 2013 inflight safety video had over 11 million hits on YouTube and was seen by thousands on their flights.[277] Thames Valley Police in the U.K. used an analogy to the culturally pervasive British tea drinking as a way of explaining sexual consent in a video.[278] By desexualizing sexual consent, they removed the emotion and cultural preconceptions and made it possible for people to hear the messages in a new light. #Consent Is Everything.

Which brings us again to the doom and gloom mistake. The videos mentioned above are fun and joyful. I am not suggesting that we make light of issues or be irresponsible, but if you are always issuing dire warnings and misery, people will stop listening. "Just say no" has never worked as a strategy.[279] State the problem, of course, but most of your communication needs to be telling people what positive and easy things they can do to keep themselves and their loved ones safe. Celebrate the good. Acknowledge the dangers. Provide directive tips on how to be safe, positively, consistently, and repetitively. Stop. Don't drink and drive. Fasten your seatbelt. Always swim near a lifeguard.

Earth Hour started in 2007 and has since grown to include more than 172 countries. The concept which was developed and launched by World Wildlife Fund is simple: ask people to turn off the lights for one hour to demonstrate a commitment to fighting climate change.[280] What has made it successful is the simplicity of the gesture, which is backed up by #YourPower and a movement that harnesses crowd power, and is reinforced by support from world leaders and celebrities, with iconic buildings such as the Eiffel Tower, the Elizabeth Tower (Big Ben), and the Sydney Opera House going dark for that hour. The World Wildlife Fund could have kept it all about them, but instead they made it an uplifting, open-source movement with an independent nonprofit and with a freestanding website. They celebrate the outcome visually with videos to demonstrate the impact of individuals working together for change.

HeForShe is a solidarity campaign for gender equality initiated by UN Women.[281] They are clear and concise in their goal and their approach: "Our mission is gender equality. Our stories make it matter. Our actions make it real."[282] On their website, they count the number of people who have committed to "Stand Together" (three billion conversations). They provide a way for people to "Track Your Impact" to find #HeForShe commitments and equality issues in each country. They encourage healthy competition by naming commitment leaders and showing high, medium, and low activity by country. They provide a simple way to "Take Action" by telling people what they can do in matters related to education, health, identity, work, violence, and politics. They launched 10x10x10 with ten key decision-makers in government, corporations, and universities around the world to drive change from the top. And they enlisted *Harry Potter* alum and UN Women Goodwill Ambassador Emma Watson as a key spokesperson.

Think of your campaign as a recipe. Ruth Reichl's boeuf à la bourguignonne (beef stew in a burgundy wine sauce) is one of my favorites.[283] It has a fairly long list of ingredients, requires several hours of prep work, plus two days of marinating, and culminates in three hours of slow cooking. It isn't something you toss together – it requires planning and time – but it is worth the effort as each individual ingredient is transformed into something truly magnificent when blended together.

You start with the diverse ingredients. (Organizations and individuals with common interests.) The ingredients can stand on their own or be used in different recipes, but together they take on a new dimension and balance each other to create something superb. The main ingredient, the beef, is the issue. The beef on its own can be a bit tough and hard to swallow, so you begin to add the supporting components. The wine tenderizes and adds depth of flavor. (Positive behavior change.) A splash of cognac adds an edge to the smoothness of the wine. (The emotions of victims and families of victims add intensity and urgency to the theoretical.) The sweetness of the carrots offset the piquancy of the onion. (Academics work with the people developing programs to balance ideals with reality and to instill best practice into common practice.) Herbs and spices provide individual flavors that interact and meld with the other ingredients. (Individual community programs to support the change.)

And then it marinates. Each individual ingredient adapts, absorbs, and begins to work with the other ingredients. This is the time when you are searching for common ground and identifying where there are conflicts of interest. At this point, you may have to temporarily separate the components, not as individuals, but as groups, to develop strategies for sharing information, adjusting program approaches, and correcting any imbalance. In our recipe analogy, this is where the liquid is in one pot, the vegetables in another, and the meat in another. There will be interventions to adjust the intensity of each ingredient or component. The beef is browned – you put your perceptions of the issue through the fire, taking a harder and more realistic look at how the issue needs to be presented. The vegetables are cooked together to meld the flavors and create a more unified approach. The wine is boiled to remove the intoxicating (overconfident and untested) effect and make it ready for wider public consumption. The spices are checked and rebalanced. And then you put the whole thing in a single pot, add a totally new flavor, the bacon, (the marketing campaign) and let it cook. Slowly, over low heat, stirring occasionally. At the very end, you add the sautéed mushrooms (social media), which absorb the flavors of all the ingredients while adding a different flavor and texture. Serve with boiled potatoes and crusty bread to best absorb the sauce (the strategic partnerships that are different but complementary). Serve and enjoy, because the whole is always greater than the sum of its parts.

Great food doesn't just happen – it requires the right chef (leader), just as social change requires a leader who can identify the strengths and weaknesses of each component, and who can visualize how everything works together. Unfortunately, visionaries are not thick on the ground and are generally first identified by far less flattering terms – annoying, interfering, stubborn, unrealistic, dangerous, radical, destructive, and crazy, to name but a few. Visionaries are usually identified as such after the fact, after what they are saying has become obvious to everyone else.

Look at movements and companies that have done it well, whether or not you agree with their focus. Anton Cermak, father of the formidable Chicago political machine, created a "house for all peoples."[284] Blake Mycoskie, founder of Tom's Shoes, with his radical business model of One for One which helps someone in need with each product purchased, started with buy-one-donate-one shoes and is now funding mental healthcare.[285] Steve Jobs. Henry Ford. Rosalind Brewer. Nelson Mandela. Tricia Griffith. Warren Buffett. There are many articles and books that dissect the attributes of visionaries. Don't limit yourself to positive role models though. It may be uncomfortable to study visionaries who have pushed abhorrent and damaging agendas, like Adolph Hitler, Joseph Stalin, Jim Jones, or Charles Manson. Even though their techniques were used for evil, they worked, so it is important to understand how they were able to influence people. Again, the purpose of this book is to identify techniques that work to harness them for positive change. Understanding these techniques also provides a playbook for undermining your competition by fighting fire with fire.

Chapter 9 Worksheet

1. What are your key messages? List all the messages.
   a. Narrow it down to five key messages.
   b. Narrow it down to three key messages.
   c. What is the single most important message?
   d. How will this single message change attitudes and behaviors?
   e. Does the message include an action verb?
   f. Is the message positive and simple?
2. Test your three key messages. Did your audience understand what behavior change is needed? If not, rewrite your messages.
3. What supporting information do your key messages require? How can you communicate these messages simply and repetitively?
4. Who are the influencers in your field? How can you market your cause to your influencers? What audience do you want your influencers to reach?
5. Who are the connectors in your field? How can you market your cause to your connectors? What audience do you want your connectors to reach?
6. What research supports your three key messages? How can you integrate that research into behavioral change?
7. What social media platforms are most used by your target audience? What type of content does your audience want? How are they engaging? How can you adapt your content?
8. Build your recipe.
   a. What are your ingredients (organizations and individuals with common interests)?
   b. What is the main ingredient (the issue)?
   c. What is your common ground?
   d. Separate the ingredients (organizations/individuals)

and re-evaluate. Adjust the spices (commitment, approach).

   e. Put your approach to the fire – are you realistic about your approach?

   f. Is your approach ready for public consumption?

   g. How does the marketing campaign bring it all together?

   h. What social media is needed?

9. Who are your visionary leaders?

Chapter 10

LOCK IN
THE CHANGE

And yet in our world everyone thinks of changing
humanity, but nobody thinks of changing himself.

Leo Tolstoy[286]

Much of the hard work has been done by this point. The foundations of change have been built. Camaraderie, excitement, peer pressure, and a sense of urgency make behavior change seem desirable. But the seductive emotion of success lulls you into a false sense of security that you have been heard and the need for change is understood. You let down your guard, move on to other things, and the competition sneaks back in and takes over. Without the right support and follow-up, all that hard work can fall apart.

It is hard to make behavior change stick. Behavior that sticks means that you stay with the new behavior even when no one is looking. Even when there are other choices. Even when the previous choice is right in front of you. Real change requires real behavior change.

In this chapter, we will look at how to create and sustain behavioral change. We will explore how attitudes influence behaviors, and vice versa. We will identify the differences between behaviors and habits and learn which to target. We will investigate the research behind behavior change and consider how you can integrate useful techniques into your approach. Humans are experts at justifying our attitudes and behaviors, so we will also explore cognitive dissonance – what it is and how it impedes or propels behavior change. Once the seeds for change are planted, momentum can take over and spread organically, just like a virus. We will therefore find out how to use behavioral contagion to our advantage.

Perhaps more than anything else in this book, realize that everything described in this chapter is being done to you every single day by friends, family, colleagues, corporations, and non-profits. Even your brain uses these techniques to shape and change you. Being aware of what is being done to you, and how, is the first step in understanding how to create positive change on a big scale, and how to combat negative change.

There are no one-size-fits-all rules for creating and reinforcing new behaviors. The jury is still out on exactly what works and why, but current research does provide us with some techniques that are more likely to work. The first step is deciding whether you want to change attitudes, behaviors, or habits. There are subtle but important differences between the three. Attitudes are feelings, beliefs, or opinions. Behaviors are "the way in which someone conducts oneself or behaves".[287] Habits are "a settled tendency or usual manner of behavior" – you act or react in the same way when prompted, every time.[288]

Advertising, media, and marketing all operate on the premise that if we change attitudes, behavior change will follow. The idea that we should focus on changing attitudes first is pervasive and has been shown to be effective, but behavior can also change attitudes. This appears to be particularly true with children and teenagers.

Children are more likely to copy the actions of others and develop attitudes based on behavior.[289] Young teenagers are more influenced by the behaviors of others in forming and changing their own attitudes.[290]

Targeting attitudes or behaviors requires you to understand your audience. Suppose you want to convince people to wear a life jacket while boating. If the target audience is parents, your primary goal will be to change their attitude about life jackets and expect the behavior change to follow. First, you provide the facts about how many lives are saved using life jackets, invoking emotions about protecting their family. Start with the attitude, then reinforce the behavior by providing information and easy access to life jackets where boats are sold and used. However, if you are trying to convince adolescents to wear life jackets, you will want to focus on changing behavior first and attitudes second. Identify adolescent influencers and convince them to wear and post photos of themselves on social media wearing life jackets while living the good life. Exhibit the behavior first and expect the attitude change to follow.

The next distinction is to decide whether you want to change a behavior or instill a habit. It is a fine line. For example, behavior is occasionally having a glass of wine when you are with friends, while habit is lighting up a cigarette every time you have a glass of wine (the prompt). The sometimes behavior of drinking a glass of wine always prompts the cigarette habit. Behavior is usually driving at the speed limit, while habit is fastening your seat belt every time you get in the car (the prompt). In the first example, if your goal is to reduce smoking, and your research shows a strong correlation between drinking and smoking, aim to create a new habit in response to the prompt of a glass of wine. Create an unconscious consistent action in response to the same prompt through the formation of a new, healthier habit, like automatically substituting olives to accompany your drink. In the second example, if your goal is safer driving, you don't necessarily want to create a habit of always driving exactly at the speed limit. Heavy traffic or poor weather warrant decreased speed. Accelerating rapidly beyond the limit may be necessary to avoid a collision or safely merge onto a highway. You want to create behavior around the principles of safe driving, but you don't want to create the habit of never deviating from the speed limit. When developing programs to change behaviors or habits, be clear on whether the action should be an unconscious reaction to a set stimulus every time. It makes a difference in how you encourage and support change.

Behavior change beyond forming a habit is rarely a straight line and can take many years.[291] A 2009 study found that on average it takes 66 days to form a new habit. It could take anywhere from 18 days up to 254 days, but plan on about two months of reinforcement for a new behavior to become a habit.[292] More difficult habit changes may take longer, and some groups are more resistant to changing habits than others. Backsliding for a day doesn't reduce the chance of forming a habit. Despite these caveats, we know that persistence pays off when it comes to creating habits.

Sixty-six days is not long when you have the big picture in mind, but the research provides a sobering reminder that even changing habits takes time and requires persistence, repetitive messaging, consistent prompts for new habits, and ongoing support. One brilliant social media post won't do it. A bracelet or ribbon won't do it. A few creative mailings won't do it. In our eight-second attention span culture, 66 days is an eternity.[293] Even more concerning, our collective attention span, our ability to focus on one topic, is diminishing rapidly as we are inundated with information from multiple sources.[294] Changing a habit is likely to be more difficult now than at any previous time in history.

For the sake of simplicity, we will use the word "behavior" throughout this chapter, as we have throughout the book, since the end goal should always be sustainable behavior change. Attitudes can change behavior, or attitudes can be changed by behavior. Habits can form, or not. How you get to a change in behavior requires an understanding the nuances described above – the clear identification of attitudes, behaviors, and habits. Once you have used data and research to determine the behaviors you wish to change or encourage, there are a number of techniques that can be used.

Changing attitudes, behaviors, and habits all comes down to a fairly simple concept: change the environment, or the perception of the environment, and it is easier to maintain the desired behavior. Your car dings when you don't fasten your seat belt, and the change in environment ATM makes it far more likely that you will buckle up. A range of communications targeting both adolescents and their parents about the consequences of breaking driving rules changes their perception of the environment. Few teenagers, or their tired-of-car-pooling parents, want to lose their brand-new license for 24 months.

Psychologist and behaviorist B. F. Skinner's famous "Skinner boxes" demonstrated that the behavior of rats could be manipulated both positively and negatively.[295] In the positive experience, when the rat pushed a bar, the reward was food. The rat quickly learned that pushing the bar created a positive experience. In the negative experience, the rat was exposed to an uncomfortable electrical current in the floor which would disappear when the rat pushed a bar. The rat quickly learned that pushing the bar eliminated the negative experience. In both cases, operant conditioning occurred – voluntary responses when placed in a defined environment.

It is uncomfortable to equate ourselves with lab rats, but think about all the situations in which we humans are trained to act. A red light appears when you are driving and you stop. You put your debit card in an ATM and money appears. The phone rings and you answer. All are examples of positive operant conditioning, which can be used to change behavior in any number of spheres. Positive operant conditioning occurs only when positive responses happen consistently, or our behavior may change again. With the rise of robocalls, perhaps you have changed your behavior and stopped answering the phone.

Negative operant conditioning means that something is taken away, and it can occur directly or as a result of inconsistencies in positive conditioning. It doesn't take many instances of grabbing a hot pan from the stove and burning yourself before you remember to use a hot pad to protect your hand. If your beloved consistently returns your affection, you are more likely to continue expressing affection because of positive operant conditioning. However, if your beloved pushes you away often enough, they are unlikely to remain your beloved for long. Occasional negative operant conditioning overrides the positive experiences.

The operant conditioning theory is not perfect. Brain disfunction can interfere with conditioning. This can include mental illness, autism, dementia, brain damage resulting from injury, disruption in brain development due to poverty or environmental factors, and adolescence. Addictive behaviors like smoking, drugs, and excessive drinking are prime examples of brain dysfunction behaviors in which the short-term hit is perceived by the brain as positive, outweighing the many long-term damaging effects. It would be hard to find a smoker these days who was not aware of the negative impact of smoking, but the behavior continues. It is harder yet to find someone who wishes to be a drug addict, but drug addiction continues. Teenagers' brains and risk assessment is another area where the operant conditioning theory falls apart. Ask a teenager why they engage in particularly baffling behavior and "I don't know!" is a common response. The adolescent brain, up to age 25, works differently from the adult brain and is guided more by emotions and reaction than by thoughtful logic.[296]

The theory is also not perfect because humans are not perfect. We are bargaining with our brains all the time, especially when the correct behavior is new, uncomfortable, unfamiliar, or infrequent. We regularly minimize the probability of potentially terrible consequences if we never experience them. The use of life jackets in boats is a perfect example. Most parents would require their young child to wear a life jacket without question but keep their own life jacket nearby "if I need it." This defeats the whole purpose, since the danger you are avoiding is entering the water unexpectedly – "unexpectedly" being the key word. If the boat capsizes or is swamped, you won't have time to put on your life jacket, anymore than you have advance warning to put on your seat belt just before a car crashes.

Some challenges are structural and require significant long-term social change, while some require short-term emergency measures. The recent COVID-19 pandemic exposed the weaknesses in existing healthcare systems, the wide variation in government responses, and the importance of coordinated global effort, but the immediate challenge was to change individual behavior in a very short time span to prevent the spread of the virus. Think of the negotiations your own brain conducted. The bargaining. The denial. Our response to the uncertainty was all over the map as we balanced what we heard with what we believed was important to us in our everyday lives, complicated by a deluge of new information as the latest research and evidence was released.

From the unwilling-to-leave-the-house, to the cautious, to the very relaxed, to the who-cares-party-on, reactions to the pandemic were interpreted individually. I wore a mask in public places, except when I walked the dog, provided I stayed at least 20 feet away from everyone. I would get a haircut, but I wouldn't go to the dentist. If I looked at my responses honestly, logic had less sway in my calculations than emotion. As an introvert, staying home or maintaining distance was no real sacrifice. I am vain enough that I wanted my hair cut properly, but I was happy to have an excuse to postpone the dentist. Logic has very little place in decision-making, even less so during uncertain times. As we saw in Chapter 1, the neuroscientist Jill Bolte Taylor said, "Although many of us think of ourselves as thinking creatures who feel, biologically we are really feeling creatures who think."[297] The importance of that statement cannot be understated.

We are in constant negotiation with our brains to justify our attitudes and behaviors. In under one second, we decide if something is "good" or "bad." Good or bad can morph into the extremes of "always or never" or "all or nothing." There is a small percentage of the population who truly thrive on extremes, people who relish high levels of conflict, who gravitate towards extreme sports, or who are susceptible to other risky behaviors, which send shots of dopamine to the pleasure center of the brain.[298] The majority of the population is more moderate. This would suggest that more moderate efforts to change attitudes and behaviors should be used, which is the view backed up by research: "If we want someone to develop a strong attitude, we should use the smallest reward or punishment that is effective in producing the desired behavior."[299] Less is more when it comes to changing behavior. Yet, it seems that we are gravitating more towards extremes every year, especially with the anonymity of social media providing a simultaneously risk-free and unrestrained platform. It may feel that extreme change is more effective, but it is not.

Research shows that extremes don't work in the way we expect. Strong (extreme) rewards, like paying your child for good grades, can backfire or work only in the short term.[300] While you may change their behavior with good grades in the short term, it is likely that their brain will rebel and adopt the attitude and future behavior that it isn't worth studying or working without immediate financial reward. Strong (extreme) punishments also tend to backfire and can cause lasting mental health damage.[301] Banning your teenager from all social media for one transgression is more likely to lead to them hunkering down and figuring out how to get around your rules, with far more detrimental outcomes. In both cases, it is very likely that the child or teen started with a moderate desire to do well in school, to receive approval from their parents, and to fit into society, but imposing extremes forced their brain to justify more excessive behaviors. The same mental gymnastics applies to adults. When we are confronted with extremes, we are more likely to change our attitudes and behaviors to fit those extremes.

Extremism manipulates formerly moderate attitudes and behaviors. Opposition to a widely supported call for common-sense gun law reform is successfully marketed as "they are coming to take *all* your guns!" Some of the same 96% of Americans who favor background checks predictably engage in outraged social media posts, panicked gun purchases, and stalking the streets with multiple weapons – the response equivalent of banning your teenager from social media.[302]

The concept of universal basic income incites fear that giving money to people, regardless of employment, will discourage them from working. Research suggests that this is likely to be true if the amount is too much – the equivalent of paying your child for good grades. Research also suggests that setting an amount which is enough to eliminate the need to choose between paying for either rent or food motivates people to work more and improves the overall economy. In other words, the idea is sound; it is the optimal moderate amount that merits debate.[303]

In both these examples, the extreme messaging has been very effective in deflecting away from the reasoned discussion, compromise, and negotiated solutions which would benefit society. Divisiveness aided and abetted by extremism fractures societies. The use of extremism in behavior change is tempting because of the apparent success, but it is also a bit like creating Frankenstein's monster. It is easy to lose control when extreme behaviors are encouraged.

The debate over guns is well trod and is a textbook example of how extremism has been used effectively. The extremist argument against a universal baseline income is new and poses an interesting test of bait and switch – a moderate attitude manipulated to become a fanatical attitude. I believe the technique is being used intentionally and is a good example of how the same tools that we can use for social good can also be used to damage society. The extreme marketing of a universal basic income is designed, in part, to divert the public's attention away from the real problem of glaring wealth inequality, including paying the tech bros, Wall Street, CEOs, and their ilk far beyond the actual value of their work to society and ultimately limiting innovation and growth for most people. Innovation means doing something that has never been done before. True innovation comes from taking risks. The willingness to take risks diminishes if there is the perception that immediate financial rewards no longer exist or are proportionally too small to merit that risk. When there is a large amount of wealth concentrated in a small number of hands, the social risk of leaving the club of the gilded few is one that few are willing to take. Despite the bombastic talk about radical change among the privileged club members, the reality is tame conformation – more tweaking than overturning.

If you want to create sustainable behavioral change, go with moderation. Extreme language is used in all fields for many purposes. Find the examples that exist in your area of interest and understand how they are negatively impacting behavior, but resist the urge to use extreme language yourself as a counterbalance.

There will always be resistance to change. Some of the most dramatic mental gymnastics occurs when we are resolving cognitive dissonance. Cognitive dissonance is "The discomfort that occurs when we behave in ways that we see as inappropriate, such as when we fail to live up to our own expectations."[304] It occurs when we are forced to comply with a new behavior, make difficult choices, or exert a significant amount of effort. Put simply, our brains don't like conflict, so our brain resolves the conflict for us.

Cognitive dissonance was first identified by Leon Festinger when he was studying a cult whose members believed the Earth would be destroyed by a flood.[305] Those who were deeply committed to the cult decided that the Earth was not destroyed because of their actions and beliefs, thus resolving their cognitive dissonance without recognizing that their underlying beliefs were flawed. The fringe members did recognize that their beliefs were flawed and moved on – there was no need to resolve any cognitive dissonance because the beliefs weren't strongly held. The more deeply held the belief system, the more strongly we adapt our thinking to hold onto our beliefs.

We encounter and resolve cognitive dissonance on a regular basis, in varying degrees. For instance, I love to travel, to the extent that I once slept on the floor for three years to fund my travel habit when my sleeper sofa broke (I had already sold my bed to fund my trips). I also care deeply about reversing the damage of the climate emergency. I know that aviation is responsible for 2.5% of global emissions,[306] so my love of travel and my desire to reverse the breakdown of the climate creates strong cognitive dissonance. I use all the tactics to reduce cognitive dissonance in a Simone Biles-worthy mental gymnastics display. I donate to organizations that plant trees to balance the impact when I fly. I have installed solar panels and use energy efficient appliances (reduce the importance of beliefs – take counteractive measures). I take a train, when possible, instead of shorter flights, and avoid business travel (change existing beliefs – I can still travel personally as long as I fly less). I virtuously decide to eat less meat, noting that livestock contributes almost 18% to greenhouse gases (add new beliefs – reducing cow burps is the real problem).[307] I have reduced my cognitive dissonance to a comfortable level. Notice that I did not mention eliminating flying for personal travel, a deeply held belief and value.

The same techniques we use individually to reduce cognitive dissonance are also used on a wider scale. The "culture wars" are very effective in weaponizing techniques to reduce cognitive dissonance to establish ever more extreme views which are harder to dislodge. Companies use marketing to reduce your cognitive dissonance to avoid radical changes to their profitable business models. When you purchase an airline ticket, you are offered the chance to make a donation to offset the carbon impact of your flight, as opposed to the industry investing heavily in innovative new technology or governments expanding public transportation. Facing increasing public and legislative grumbling, Facebook began an ad campaign for targeted audiences outlining their support for legislation "combating foreign election interference, protecting people's privacy, and enabling safe and easy data portability between platforms"[308] — that is, deflecting and delaying responsibility, as opposed to simply changing their platform and business model without legislation. Alcohol companies have launched "drink responsibly" campaigns ever since MADD so effectively took on drunk driving, as opposed to addressing the 10% of American drinkers who are buying more than half of all alcohol.[309] If it looks like a bait-and-switch campaign, it is probably an attempt to reduce cognitive dissonance to distract from the real change that is needed.

Again, the tactics to reduce cognitive dissonance are about reducing the importance of beliefs, changing existing beliefs, and adding new beliefs. You will also need to assess the strength of any existing beliefs before deciding on a counterstrategy. What appears to be hypocrisy can be a clue to existing cognitive dissonance. More subtle cognitive dissonance can be more difficult to uncover. Follow the whys to break down the belief system, find the underlying beliefs, and identify how strongly they are held.

Beyond extremism and deeply held beliefs, most resistance to change comes when people think they will lose something of value or don't understand the implications of the change and how it may benefit them. They resist change to protect their self-interest. We humans are limited in our ability to change, so fear of change will always be a barrier.

We can learn some of the best techniques for overcoming resistance to change from the business world. John Kotter and Leonard Schlesinger first published the article "Choosing Strategies for Change" in 1979, but it remains one of the most coherent and helpful summaries.[310] Education and communication top the list. Engage. Talk it through. Make the effort. Listen. Invest in discussions, presentations, surveys, and focus groups. Too often, this step is discouraged as "soft" or not fast enough, but education and communication are the most effective tools for behavioral change in every single field. I firmly believe that early childhood education is the answer to most of the world's ills, a belief supported by ample research. However, education isn't fast, glamorous, appealing to venture capitalists, or profitable, so it is often neglected.[311] It isn't surprising that education is less valued because we also assign less value to educators. Some 63% of teachers in the United States are female, resulting in a historically underpaid and under-appreciated workforce.[312] Or, as a school committee in Littleton, Massachusetts stated in 1849, when it was determined that all children should be educated, why pay men $20 a month when "a female could do the work more successfully at one third of the price"?[313] Identify internal biases against education before favoring a flashier approach.

Participation and involvement follow along the same lines. Engage and listen through education and communication, then get people on board with participating in the change. Find leaders and influencers in your target audience and enlist them as ambassadors for change. When people have skin in the game, they are more likely to believe in, and adopt, the change. It is all part of resolving cognitive dissonance.

Facilitation and support are necessary for any change. As we saw earlier, changing the environment to support the change is key, as is providing ongoing support for the change. This may be especially important if fear or anxiety is preventing the change, but all behavior change will be attained more smoothly if you can create a supportive environment.

Negotiation and agreement may be used sparingly, but only with plenty of education or it can backfire. For instance, if a local government wants to update their recycling to include food scraps, and there is community concern about the smell of rotting food or attracting pests between the regular scheduled pick-ups, the local government may negotiate more frequent food recycling pick-ups or supply special no-odor pest-proof containers, but even these alternatives won't work without education and communication.

The techniques of manipulation, co-optation, and outright explicit or implicit coercion may be used but, again, they can backfire and rarely result in lasting change. These strategies are deployed more often in employment situations or authoritarian environments where the power dynamics are one-sided. Language is a useful clue; look for words like toxic, degrading, oppressive, harsh, or rigid. There is little research to support the use of these techniques for lasting behavioral change outside of situations where you have substantial control. Be aware of what techniques are being utilized and learn how to guard against them.

Manipulation involves the selective use of information and a conscious structuring of events – the creation of an alternative universe of facts. The recent trend towards labeling unwanted facts as "fake news" and discounting the science behind COVID-19 and the climate emergency are examples of manipulation. If you don't believe the scientists, then climate breakdown isn't happening or isn't that bad. A manipulator can expand their impact by co-opting others to push through beliefs and changes. The person being manipulated will resolve their cognitive dissonance by falling hook, line, and sinker for the party line, even at the expense of their own beliefs, career, or lives.

Co-opting involves encouraging people to become part of a group or system. It can have a positive slant, resulting in compliance, or a negative one, resulting in resistance.

Explicit and implicit coercion forces people to change through threats and force. Coercion is highly effective in the short term when speed is of the essence and those who wish to see change hold considerable power, as is the case with authoritarian leaders, but even they eventually lose power or die. For lasting behavioral change, coercion should only be used in rare cases, if at all.

The barriers to creating change can seem overwhelming, but momentum is on your side. Behavioral contagion operates just like a highly contagious virus. Once you have removed the obstacles for the behavioral change, your work is done. The contagion spreads organically, for better or for worse. Behavioral contagion works just as you might imagine. Just as one person sneezes and everyone around them catches a cold, so behavioral contagion is the tendency for people to repeat a behavior after they have seen others perform it.[314] We are all natural mimics. We copy each other without conscious thought – speech patterns, mannerisms, the clothes we wear. This tendency can spread both healthy and unhealthy behaviors. The most powerful predictor of whether a teenager will smoke is the percentage of their friends who smoke.[315] On the positive side, behavioral contagion to spread the word of the benefits and dramatically dropping cost of solar power is accelerating adoption, helping to address climate breakdown through the increased use of renewable energy.[316]

The best way to utilize behavioral contagion is to clearly define the desired behavior and then find influencers to demonstrate the behavior. Determine where your target audience spends their time. Use the techniques described in this chapter to change attitudes, behaviors, and habits with the goal of planting the seeds, preparing the environment for change, and then watching behavioral contagion do the work for you.

You don't have to do this alone. All social change requires a movement, so find your people. As Benjamin Franklin said, "We must all hang together, or assuredly we shall all hang separately."[317]

Chapter 10 Worksheet

Attitudes = feelings, beliefs, or opinions
Behaviors = actions or reactions
Habits = act or react the same way, when prompted, every time

1. Do you want to change an attitude or behavior first?
How old is your target audience?

- Children (0–10 years) – encouraging parents and influential adults and media sources to model the desired behavior is more likely to change children's attitudes.
- Young adolescents (10–15 years) – encouraging parents and influential adults and media sources to model the desired behavior is more likely to change the attitudes of young teens.
- Older adolescents (16–25 years) – use a blend of changing attitudes and behaviors through modeling behavior by respected peers and adults, and changing attitudes through education, awareness, and influencers.
- Adults (26 years and older) – focus on changing attitudes through education, awareness, and influencers. Behavior change will follow.

2. Do you want to change a behavior or instill a habit?

- Habit – you want your audience to act in exactly the same way, in response to the same prompt, every single time.
    - It takes an average of 66 days to form a habit. During this time, repeatedly and

consistently provide the exact prompt with a reminder of the correct action (habit).
- Focus on creating an environment that reinforces the correct action.
- Establish a supportive environment while the habit is created – education, communication, support, mentoring, providing cues, and removing obstacles.
- Behavior – you want your audience to change their actions in response to the environment.
  - Behavior change can take several years.
  - Establish a supportive environment until the behavior is internalized – education, communication, support, mentoring, providing cues, and removing obstacles

3. Will positive or negative operant conditioning help to reinforce behavior change?

   - Positive change is typically more sustainable. Identify positive supports for behavior change.
   - Identify negative behavior reinforcements, especially when they may save lives (e.g. traffic fines).

4. Appeal to emotions more than logic.

   - Logical reasons for change.
   - Emotional reasons for change.
   - Logical reasons which can be reframed as emotional reasons.

5. Analyze the language you are currently using. Do you use extreme statements – "all or nothing," "always or never," "good and bad"?

    - Extreme statements.
    - Alternative statements.
    - Does your competition use extreme statements? How can you undermine their statements, cast doubt, or diffuse their arguments?
    - Extreme statements.
    - Diffused statements.

6. Identify the cognitive dissonance that exists in your target audience – the conflict that occurs when we are forced to comply with a new behavior, make difficult changes, or exert a significant amount of effort.

    - Cognitive dissonance.
    - Identify strategies for reducing cognitive dissonance with the new behavior.
    - Reduce the importance of beliefs.
    - Change existing beliefs.
    - Add new beliefs.

7. Most resistance to change comes when people think they will lose something of value or don't understand the implications of the change and how it may benefit them.

    - Education and communication.
    - Participation and involvement.
    - Facilitation and support.
    - Negotiation and agreement.

- Techniques of manipulation and co-optation and outright explicit or implicit coercion can be used, but they are of limited value and have a higher potential of backfiring. Identify areas where you are using these techniques and develop alternative strategies.
- Manipulation, co-optation, coercion.
- Alternative strategies.

8. Behavior change is most easily spread like a contagious virus.

- Look at your target audience. Who influences them? Among the influencers, who are your potential super-spreaders?
- Can you engage with these potential super-spreaders?
- How can you convince the influencers to become super-spreaders? Which of their emotions do you need to engage?

Chapter 11

WHEN TO BUILD AND WHEN TO BAIL

Should you find yourself in a chronically leaking boat,
energy devoted to changing vessels is likely to be more
productive than energy devoted to patching leaks.

Attributed to Warren Buffett[318]

It is hard to know when to hold the course, when to change direction, and when to bail out. Since activists, by definition, act, knowing when to pivot can be especially challenging.

Activists are passionate people. Regardless of where you fall on the political or cultural spectrum, no one becomes an activist unless they feel strongly enough about an issue to act. Strength of conviction can move mountains. Strength of conviction can also destroy you if you are too rigid to adapt to changing circumstances or new information.

The two classes in academia that had the greatest impact on me were "Negotiations" and "Power and Politics." It is no exaggeration to say that I have used what I learned in those classes every day of my life. Too often, we equate winning with bludgeoning our opponent and pushing through our point of view and belief system, the consequences be damned. One of the most influential books on war, written sometime between 475 and 221 BCE was *The Art of War* by Sun Tzu, who is believed to have been a brilliant general.[319] This book was one of the textbooks for my "Power and Politics" class. The advice is still studied and used by modern-day military and corporate leaders.

If you do a quick online search for quotes from the book (and they are legion), you will see that Sun Tzu understood that the ability to continually assess and pivot was key to success: "Hold out baits to entice the enemy. Feign disorder, and crush him." "If he is secure at all points, be prepared for him. If he is in superior strength, evade him." "If your opponent is of choleric temper, seek to irritate him. Pretend to be weak, that he may grow arrogant." "Attack him where he is unprepared, appear where you are not expected."[320]

The same principle holds with negotiations. *Getting to Yes: Negotiating Agreement Without Giving In* by Roger Fisher and William Ury was my primary textbook.[321] The crucial point I took away was always to identify your BATNA – your best alternative negotiated agreement. Look at your most desirable outcome, the point where you will walk away from the negotiating table, having found a middle ground where both partners give a little, but both end up better than they were before. The middle ground is your BATNA. Successfully achieving your goal without anyone dying or alienating potential future partners is the goal – very similar to Sun Tzu's philosophy. This undoubtedly stems from one of the key (often forgotten) principles of business, drummed into me throughout business school: it is far more profitable to look after existing customers than to ignore them and constantly look for new customers. Partnership and collaboration are winning strategies. It has been decades since I took the class, but the idea still stands, with recent data showing that acquiring a new client costs between five and seven times more than retaining an existing client and increasing client retention increases profits by 25%–95%.[322]

The data is clear. Reaching agreement is profitable. Fighting to the death or crushing your opponent is not profitable. Profit in social change is measured in lives improved or saved, communities enhanced, conservation achieved, violence reduced, or money saved. Focusing on collaboration and partnership is similar to focusing on prevention rather than cure – the returns far exceed the investment. Every $1 invested in early childhood yields a $4–$16 return in terms of increased high school graduation, college matriculation, economic development, and personal income, and decreased special education/remediation, dependence on social welfare, and crime-related costs and incarceration rates.[323] Teaching a child the Swim to Survive curriculum costs $13.46–$30,[324] but the cost of caring for a child who has brain damage from a nonfatal drowning incident ranges from hundreds of thousands to millions of dollars over their lifetime. Those outcomes are "profits" in social change terms and in hard dollars.

The concepts of partnership, collaboration, and positive change sound almost quaint given the bellicose nature of many world leaders in recent years, not to mention the actions of some corporate leaders. Even the most heinous are regularly pivoting. They may be learning from the actions of other autocrats, narcissists, sociopaths, and thugs, but they are pivoting nonetheless. If citizens and medical facilities can be decimated without impunity in one country (Syria), try it in another country (Ukraine). If women can be silenced and stripped of all autonomy in one country (Afghanistan), try it in other countries (the United States and depressingly too many others to name).[325] Call the legitimacy of elections into question. Lie with a straight face by calling the truth "fake news," and then double down on the lie. Bait and switch by flatly refusing to answer questions about drug or alcohol abuse, involvement in human trafficking, tax evasion, bribery, and failing businesses, all while redirecting supporters' and detractors' emotions to unrelated issues. It is all pivoting, following the lessons from Sun Tzu and effective negotiations.

Refusing to employ these techniques because they are used effectively by businesses is the equivalent of maintaining an arsenal of bows and arrows against a competitor with a bomb. You don't become evil by using the same techniques; you only become evil if your intended outcome is to harm. To be an effective activist, you need to use strategies that are proven to be effective.

One of the most valuable skills I learned in consulting training was to ask, "What went well? What would you do differently next time?" I ask myself these questions for every project I complete, whether it is developing the first U.S. National Water Safety Action Plan or building shelves for the garage. In this chapter, we will look at how to evaluate all you have learned in this book and decide whether it is time to sail on, patch the boat, find a new boat, or jump ship completely.

Each chapter in this book concludes with a worksheet to help you break down how the content applies to the change you are pursuing. The worksheets are designed to dive into the details. In this last chapter, we will move from the detail to the big picture, and back down to the details.

Looking at the big picture, do you still have the same goal? Has new information from the details, implementation plan, or partnerships shifted your big goal? Have unforeseen consequences changed the details or the big picture? Have you achieved your initial goal and need to focus on the next step? Has the problem been solved?

Use the worksheets at the end of each chapter to evaluate the details. Write a brief summary of each worksheet answering the following questions.

1. Have you identified the real problem – the underlying problem?
2. Look at your whys. What are the underlying causes of the issue? Do you want to address these underlying causes?

Who is impacted? Who else needs to be involved in the why discussion? Can you collaborate? What if the people impacted won't collaborate? What if the divisions are too deep? Are the barriers to collaborating with you or with others? Do you want to change?

3. Identify the puzzle pieces. Looking at the big picture, where do you fit in? What are the variables? Identify the competition, target audience, influencers, roadblocks, and conflicts of interest. Identify the components of research, action, and emotion – are they working together effectively?

4. Do you agree with the story the data is telling you? If not, are you resistant to the change that needs to happen? What is the data capturing? What is the data not capturing? Is the data being ignored? How do you market what the data is telling you to the right audience?

5. Follow the money. How can you use data to create financial arguments for your program? How will you use data to tell your story? Don't rely on data to tell your story – what is your emotional hook? Where are your stories?

6. Focusing on data-driven solutions creates an intrinsic bias and limits creativity. How does that look in your field? What programs could help to increase your data fluency? What innovations in data are needed?

7. Data alone doesn't change behavior. You need to:
    - Identify the desired change.
    - Communicate the desired change. Find the one thing you want your audience to remember. It is never the audience that is the problem; it is always the message.
    - Model the desired change.
    - Measure both the intended and unintended outcomes.

- Continually assess whether the desired change is achieving your goal.
8. Find your target audience.
9. What are your three key messages? What is the behavior change you hope to see? What are the consequences of not changing behavior? How deep do you have to dig to create educated instinct? Are you the right person or organization to reach the audience? Test your message on a subset of your target audience.
10. What societal norms are in place that support current behaviors? How deeply do these norms run? Do they make sense today?

Once you have written summaries of your worksheets, read them out loud. Yes, out loud. When you read silently, it tends to sound more logical and rational than when it is exposed to oxygen and the human ear. Is there anything that doesn't make sense in that first reading? Are any details working against each other?

Now, read the summary again in the context of your big goal. Do the details support your big goal? What needs to change to adapt to your new approach or to pivot? Is there a detail that would substantially influence your final stay-the-course or pivot decision? Are the details the right tools to help you reach your big goal? If not, what needs to change in the big picture or in the details?

Evaluate whether you are headed in the right direction, need a course correction, or whether it is time to abandon ship. This exercise will prevent you from wasting time and resources.

Perhaps the hardest questions to ask yourself include, are you the right person? Is this the right fight? Is this the right time? Your passion and skills are needed. Whether your passion is helping an individual, your local community, or the world, you *can* change the world, and you *can* make a difference. Better that you are applying your passion and skills where they can do the most good and where you get the greatest satisfaction.

At least once a year, ask yourself the following tough questions.

- What type of activist are you? Does this type of activism play to your strengths, or did you get pulled into a role because you are amazing, talented, and reliable? What are you doing now? Does it fit your personality? Do you feel "flow" when you are engaged – that addictive dopamine hit to the brain where you are firing on all cylinders and the words and actions flow – or are you going through the motions? What type of activist do you want to become? Will your current role allow you to reach your full potential, or are you being held back?

- There is no shame in saying "not for me," but it is a shame if your full talents aren't being put to good use. Change won't happen unless we are using the best people and resources in the right roles. Don't waste your talents on "someone needs to do it" or "we need a warm body in the role." Evaluate whether your passion and skills are being used for optimum impact. Yes, we all must do drudgery occasionally, but aim for drudgery being the exception, not the rule.

- Do you have the right skills to accomplish your goals? Do you need to find a collaborator? Where do you fit in the details from the worksheets? Are you in the right role, or is it time to switch? Do you want to learn new skills, or should you move to a position that allows you to use the skills you have? Are you open to changing yourself, or are you resistant to change?

- Do you still have the passion, or are you burned out and jaded? Recognizing that it is time to move on is one of the hardest things to do. Many activists, business owners, and leaders stay in their position for too long. Perhaps they believe their own hype – that only they can save the world – even if they cannot physically and mentally keep up. Perhaps they believe that their way, their initial vision, is the one right way to run an organization or campaign or serve in a position. If you find yourself thinking, "this is the way we've always done it," or "no one else understands or does it better," or you feel resentment and resistance towards others, it is almost certainly time to pivot. If you aren't bringing new talent into your board or organization, forming new partnerships, or regularly reaching outside your field to collaborate on parallel issues (like drowning prevention campaigners collaborating with climate activists), you are dead in the water or floating backwards. Perhaps the emotional reasons that drew you to an issue in the first place need to be redirected in a way that still respects and honors the loss or traumatic event you experienced. Perhaps you have been trying so hard for so long that all you can see are the reasons change will never happen. You have become blind to the positive energy and possibilities that made you an activist in the first place.

You don't have to give up activism if you are burned out and cynical in your current position. If developing strategy for start-ups fires you up, but your skills mean you were promoted to the management of a large bureaucratic organization, switch back to working with start-ups. Work with multiple start-ups as a consultant, or with an organization that provides support for small organizations. Conversely, if you have ended up in the field, but developing strategy is your thing, find a big organization that needs your skills. Explore a new way of contributing by becoming a mentor or teacher. Take your skills to a different field where you can feel the passion again. A true activist wants to make a difference for as long as they can draw breath. It is so much better to feel the fire-in-the-belly, the dopamine rush to the brain when you make a difference, the excitement of engaging with like-minded people, the utter thrill of seeing change happen. Being a passive observer of life just doesn't cut it. Knowing when to pivot is the opposite of failing. Applying your skills and your passion effectively, in a way that gives you deep satisfaction, is the ultimate success.

Activism can be hard, but with the tools in this book, you will be more effective. The right tools can make all the difference. You will see more success than failure. Positive change will happen more quickly. You will utilize your own skills and those of others more appropriately, pulling the best from people and feeling greater joy from your contribution. At a time when the news tells us that the world is hopeless and we are doomed to the status quo, I am more convinced than ever that activists are the answer, that activists are the hope. Effective activism will save us. Activism that looks beyond "the way we've always done it," seizes marketing and other successful techniques from the business world and wields them like the powerful weapon for change that they are. For generations, we have been told that if we follow the rules, everything will work out. It did — for a small group that understood the power of marketing behavior change. It is our turn now. It is time for activists to rise up. It is time to take back the power and market change effectively.

I can think of no greater gift than to be an activist. To believe that change is possible, that humans are capable of great things, that each of us can change the world in our own way. Being an activist is a positive and pragmatic way to live. It is frustrating and fulfilling, challenging and invigorating, deeply individual and part of something bigger than yourself. To be an activist is to be gloriously human.

171

> We must all obey the great law of change. It is the most powerful law of nature.
>
> Edmund Burke[326]

RESOURCES

I find the world endlessly fascinating – the natural world, people, and culture. It is always a joy to have my worldview shifted by the insights and arguments of informed people, some of which are represented in this book list.

BEHAVIOR CHANGE

Jonah Berger, *The Catalyst: How to Change Anyone's Mind* (Cambridge: Social Dynamics Group, 2020).

Jeanne M. Brett, *Negotiating Globally: How to Negotiate Deals, Resolve Disputes, and Make Decisions Across Cultural Boundaries,* 3rd edn (San Francisco, CA: Jossey-Bass, 2014).

Roger Fisher and William Ury, *Getting to Yes: Negotiating Agreement Without Giving In* (Boston and New York: Houghton Mifflin, 1981).

Chip Heath and Dan Heath, *Made to Stick: Why Some Ideas Survive and Others Die* (London: Random House, 2007).

Chip Heath and Dan Heath, *Switch: How to Change Things When Change is Hard* (New York: Broadway Books, 2010).

Kerry Patterson, Joseph Grenny, David Mayfield, Ron McMillan, and Al Switzler, *Influencer: The Power to Change Anything* (New York: VitalSmarts/McGraw-Hill, 2008).

DATA

Caroline Criado Perez, *Invisible Women: Data Bias in a World Designed for Men* (London: Penguin Random House, 2019).

HEALTHCARE

Elisabeth Rosenthal, *An American Sickness: How Healthcare Became Big Business and How You Can Take It Back* (New York: Penguin, 2017).

HUMAN NATURE

Rutger Bregman, *Humankind: A Hopeful History* (London: Little, Brown and Company, 2019).

Edward Slingerland, *Drunk: How We Sipped, Danced, and Stumbled Our Way to Civilization* (London: Little, Brown Spark, 2021).

William Shakespeare, *The Complete Works of William Shakespeare.* https://www.gutenberg.org/ebooks/100

Sun Tzu, *The Art of War*, tr. Lionel Giles (Garsington: Benediction Classics, 2018).

MONEY

Ha-Joon Chang, *Economics: The User's Guide* (London: Bloomsbury Publishing, 2014).

Peter S. Goodman, *Davos Man: How the Billionaires Devoured the World* (New York: HarperCollins, 2022).

Jane Mayer, *Dark Money: The Hidden History of the Billionaires Behind the Rise of the Radical Right* (New York: Anchor Books, 2016).

SOCIAL MARKETING

Jeff French, Clive Blair-Stevens, Dominic McVey, and Rowena Merritt, *Social Marketing and Public Health: Theory and Practice* (New York: Oxford University Press, 2010).

Jeff French, Rowena Merritt, and Lucy Reynolds, *Social Marketing Casebook* (Thousand Oaks, CA: SAGE Publications, 2011).

Nancy R. Lee and Philip Kotler, *Social Marketing: Changing Behaviors for Good*, 5th edn (Thousand Oaks, CA: SAGE Publications, 2016).

ENDNOTES

1   See https://www.cdc.gov/vitalsigns/drowning/index.html

2   See https://www.who.int/news-room/fact-sheets/detail/drowning

3   See https://www.watersafetyusa.org/nwsap.html

4   See https://www.chicagowatersafety.org/. See also City of Chicago
    Lakefront Safety Task Force, *Initial Report 2018–2019* (2019),
    https://static1.squarespace.com/static/5a1396d96957dabef9f91d3b/
    t/5cabb871c83025d6b439f8ee/1554757745539/
    Chicago+Water+Safety+Report+4.8.2019.pdf

CHAPTER 1

5   Martin Luther King Jr., "Martin Luther King Jr. on the Vietnam
    War," *The Atlantic*, February 2018, https://www.theatlantic.com/
    magazine/archive/2018/02/martin-luther-king-jr-vietnam/552521/

6   Patrick R. Steffen, Dawson Hedges, and Rebekka Matheson R,
    "The Brain Is Adaptive Not Triune: How the Brain Responds to
    Threat, Challenge, and Change," *Frontiers in Psychiatry*. 2022. 13:
    802606. doi: 10.3389/fpsyt.2022.802606, https://www.ncbi.nlm.
    nih.gov/pmc/articles/PMC9010774/

7   Jennifer S. Lerner, Ye Li, Piercarlo Valdesolo, and Karim S. Kassam,
    "Emotion and Decision Making," *Annual Review of Psychology*.

2015. 66: 33.1–33.25. doi: 10.1146/annurev-psych-010213-115043, 13 September 2014, https://scholar.harvard.edu/files/jenniferlerner/files/emotion_and_decision_making.pdf/

8   Ashfaq Khalfan, Astrid N. Lewis, Carlos Aguilar, Jacqueline Persson, Max Lawson, Nafkote Dabi et al., *Climate Equality: A Planet for the 99%* (Oxford: Oxfam International, 2023), https://oxfamilibrary.openrepository.com/bitstream/handle/10546/621551/cr-climate-equality-201123-en-summ.pdf; Fred Dews, "Ten Facts About Billionaires," *Brookings Institution*, 12 September 2014, https://www.brookings.edu/articles/ten-facts-about-billionaires/

9   See https://www.cdc.gov/drowning/data-research/facts/

10   James Hamblin, "A Racial History of Drowning: So That Eventually Every Kid Learns to Swim," *The Atlantic*, 11 June 2013, https://www.theatlantic.com/health/archive/2013/06/a-racial-history-of-drowning/276748/

11   Jill Bolte Taylor, "The Neuroanatomical Transformation of the Teenage Brain: Jill Bolte Taylor at TEDxYouth@Indianapolis," 21 February 2013, *YouTube*, https://www.youtube.com/watch?v=PzT_SBl31-s/

12   Philip Kotler and Gerald Zaltman, "Social Marketing: An Approach to Planned Social Change," *Journal of Marketing*. 1971. 35(3): 3–12; see also Aiden Truss, Robert Marshall, and Clive Blair-Stevens, "A History of Social Marketing." In Jeff French, Clive Blair-Stevens, Dominic McVey, and Rowena Merritt (eds), *Social Marketing and Public Health: Theory and Practice* (New York: Oxford University Press, 2009), pp. 19–28.

13   Rebecca Masters, Elspeth Anwar, Brendan Collins, Richard Cookson, and Simon Capewell, "Return on Investment of Public Health Interventions: A Systematic Review," *Journal of Epidemiology and Community Health*. 2017. 71: 827–834, https://eprints.whiterose.ac.uk/116811/1/jech_2016_208141.full.pdf/

14   Krishna Ramanujan, "More Than 99.9% of Studies Agree: Humans Caused Climate Change," *Cornell Chronicle*, 19

October 2021, https://news.cornell.edu/stories/2021/10/more-999-studies-agree-humans-caused-climate-change/

15   See https://www.who.int/news-room/fact-sheets/detail/tobacco/

16   Ruth A. Brenner, Gitanjali Saluja Taneja, Denise L. Hayne, Ann C. Trumble, Song Qian, Ron M. Klinger, and Mark A. Klebanoff, "Association Between Swimming Lessons and Drowning in Childhood: A Case-Control Study," *Archives of Pediatric and Adolescent Medicine.* 2009. 163(3): 203–210, https://www.ncbi.nlm.nih.gov/pmc/articles/PMC4151293/

17   Gallup, "What Percentage of Americans Own Guns?" 13 November 2020, https://news.gallup.com/poll/264932/percentage-americans-own-guns.aspx/

18   See https://everytownresearch.org/issue/child-and-teens/; Stephanie Pappas, "More Than 20% of Teens Have Seriously Considered Suicide: Psychologists and Communities Can Help Tackle the Problem," *Monitor on Psychology.* 2023. 54: 5, https://www.apa.org/monitor/2023/07/psychologists-preventing-teen-suicide/; Arthur L. Kellermann, Grant Somes, Frederick P. Rivara, Roberta K. Lee, and Joyce G. Banton, "Injuries and Deaths Due to Firearms in the Home," *Journal of Trauma.* 1998. 45(2): 263–267. doi: 10.1097/00005373-199808000-00010, https://pubmed.ncbi.nlm.nih.gov/9715182/

19   See https://www.familiesunitedtopreventdrowning.org/

20   Johan Norberg, "Globalization's Greatest Triumph: The Death of Extreme Poverty," *CATO Institute*, 26 September 2018, https://www.cato.org/commentary/globalizations-greatest-triumph-death-extreme-poverty/

21   Gustave M. Gilbert, *Nuremberg Diary* (New York: Signet, 1947), p. 256, https://archive.org/details/the-nuremberg-diary-1971-gustave-gilbert/

CHAPTER 2

22   Jason D. Reynolds (Taewon Choi), Bridget M. Anton, Chiroshri

Bhattacharjee, and Megan E. Ingraham, "The Work of a Revolutionary: A Psychobiography and Careerography of Angela Y. Davis," *Europe's Journal of Psychology*. 2021. 17(3): 198–209. doi: 10.5964/ejop.5507, https://www.ncbi.nlm.nih.gov/pmc/articles/PMC8763219/

23 Carl Jung, *Psychologische Typen* (Zürich: Rascher Verlag, 1921).

24 Aquarius M. Gordon, "In Defense of the Myers–Briggs: A Comprehensive Counter to Anti-MBTI Hype," *Psychology Today*, 12 February 2020, https://www.psychologytoday.com/us/blog/my-brothers-keeper/202002/in-defense-the-myers-briggs

25 See https://www.16personalities.com/free-personality-test

26 See https://birkman.com/the-birkman-method

27 Mark Murphy, "Which of These 4 Communication Styles Are You?" *Forbes Magazine*, 6 August 2015, https://www.forbes.com/sites/markmurphy/2015/08/06/which-of-these-4-communication-styles-are-you/; Washington State Department of Enterprise Services, "Leading Teams Participant Guide: Colors Preferred Communication Style Assessment," June 2022, https://des.wa.gov/sites/default/files/2022-06/ColorsPreferredCommunicationStyleAssessment.pdf; see also https://umatter.princeton.edu/respect/tools/communication-styles

28 FindErnest, "Skill Assessment Tests – What, Why, Where, How it is Useful and Essential?" 13 March 2023, *LinkedIn*, https://www.linkedin.com/pulse/skill-assessment-tests-what-why-where-how-useful-essential/

29 Sheila Kloefkorn, "The History of Skills Testing," *eSkill Talent Assessment Platform*, 6 June 2017, https://eskill.com/blog/history-skills-testing; see also https://careers.state.gov/career-paths/foreign-service/officer/fso-test-information-and-selection-process/

30 See https://www.apa.org/topics/implicit-bias

31 Robyn Jorgensen, *Early-Years Swimming: Adding Capital to Young Australians*, August 2013, https://worldwideswimschool.com/wp-content/uploads/2017/08/2013-EYS-Final-Report-30-July-13-JM.

pdf

32 See https://www.psychologytoday.com/us/basics/groupthink

33 Quoted in Glenn Kramon, "How to Win More Games Than Anyone," *New York Times*, 14 January 2024, https://www.nytimes.com/2024/01/14/business/tara-vanderveer-stanford-basketball.html

34 Massachusetts Institute of Technology LBGTQ+ Services, "A Guide to Pronouns: A Quick History and Best Practices Video Transcript," n.d., https://lbgtq.mit.edu/sites/default/files/documents/Transcript for Website - A Guide to Pronouns_ A Quick History and Best Practices.pdf

35 See https://www.cdc.gov/suicide/disparities

36 Eric Mosley, "IBM's Culture of Transformation," *Forbes*, 2 June 2021, https://www.forbes.com/sites/ericmosley/2021/06/02/ibms-culture-of-transformation/?sh=3654c65b3482

37 Hemant Taneja, "The Era of 'Move Fast and Break Things' Is Over," *Harvard Business Review*, 22 January 2019, https://hbr.org/2019/01/the-era-of-move-fast-and-break-things-is-over

38 See https://www.jpmorganchase.com/careers/work-with-us

39 Ramon Laguarta, "Celebrating the Pepsico Way," *Pepsico Careers*, n.d., https://stories.pepsicojobs.com/blog/2020/07/01/celebrating-pepsico-culture/

40 See https://www.redcross.org/about-us/careers/culture.html

41 See https://www.goodwillsewcareers.com/about-us/mission-values

42 See https://www.amnesty.org/en/about-us

43 See https://www.stjude.org/about-st-jude.html

44 See https://www.chesterfield.gov/1005/Suicide-Awareness

45 See http://www.facesva.org

46 See https://www.chicagowatersafety.org

47 Michael Marshall, "Earliest Known War in Europe was a Stone Age Conflict 5000 Years Ago," *New Scientist*, 2 November 2023, https://www.newscientist.com/article/2400895-earliest-known-war-in-europe-was-a-stone-age-conflict-5000-years-ago/; see also

https://www.war-memorial.net/wars_all.asp; https://www.war-memorial.net/wars_all.asp; https://geneva-academy.ch/galleries/today-s-armed-conflicts

48   See https://www.usip.org/issue-areas/nonviolent-action

49   Alexander Dumas, *The Three Musketeers* (1988 [1844]), ch. 9, *Project Gutenberg*, https://www.gutenberg.org/cache/epub/1257/pg1257-images.html

50   Robert Cass Keller, "We Must All Hang Together ..." Word Ways. 1976. 9(1): 3, https://digitalcommons.butler.edu/wordways/vol9/iss1/3/

CHAPTER 3

51   Eleanor Roosevelt, *Book of Common Sense Etiquette* (New York: Macmillan, 1962), p. 16, https://archive.org/details/eleanorroosevelt0000unse_n3a5/page/16/mode/2up

52   See https://www.redcross.org/about-us/who-we-are/mission-and-values.html

53   See https://www.moma.org/about/mission-statement

54   See https://www.peacecorps.gov/what-we-do/our-mission

55   See https://www.islasurf.org

56   Pew Research Center, "Americans' Views of Government: Low Trust, But Some Positive Performance Ratings," 14 September 2020, https://www.pewresearch.org/politics/2020/09/14/americans-views-of-government-low-trust-but-some-positive-performance-ratings/; Erica Sweeney, "53% of Consumers Believe Brands Can Do More to Solve Social Problems Than Governments," *Marketing Dive*, 5 October 2018, https://www.marketingdive.com/news/53-of-consumers-believe-brands-can-do-more-to-solve-social-problems-than-g/538925/

57   See https://www.macrotrends.net/global-metrics/countries/USA/united-states/clean-water-access-statistics; World Health Organization, "Drinking Water," 13 September 2023, https://www.who.int/news-room/fact-sheets/detail/drinking-water

58 See https://www.statista.com/outlook/cmo/non-alcoholic-drinks/bottled-water/united-states

59 Melissa Denchak, "Flint Water Crisis: Everything You Need to Know," *Natural Resources Defense Council,* 8 October 2024, https://www.nrdc.org/stories/flint-water-crisis-everything-you-need-know

60 See https://www.usla.org/page/statistics

61 Shradha Dinesh and Meltem Odabaş, "8 facts About Americans and Twitter as it Rebrands to X," *Pew Research Center,* 26 July 2023, https://www.pewresearch.org/short-reads/2023/07/26/8-facts-about-americans-and-twitter-as-it-rebrands-to-x/

62 See https://www.councilofnonprofits.org/about-americas-nonprofits/economic-impact-nonprofits; Independent Sector, "Health of the U.S. Nonprofit Sector," 13 November 2023, https://independentsector.org/resource/health-of-the-u-s-nonprofit-sector/

63 "80% of Nonprofits' Revenue is from Government, Fee for Service," *Nonprofit Times,* 20 September 2019, https://thenonprofittimes.com/news/80-of-nonprofits-revenue-is-from-government-fee-for-service/

64 Julia Faria, "Advertising Spending in Hospitals," *Statista,* 12 September 2024, https://www.statista.com/statistics/470699/hospitals-industry-ad-spend-usa/

65 See https://nces.ed.gov/fastfacts/display.asp?id=73

66 See https://www.cms.gov/data-research/statistics-trends-and-reports/national-health-expenditure-data/historical

67 David Blumenthal, Evan D. Dumas, Arnav Shah, Munira Z. Gunja, and Reginald D. Williams II, "Mirror, Mirror 2024: A Portrait of the Failing U.S. Health System: Comparing Performance in 10 Nations," *Commonwealth Fund,* 19 September 2024, https://www.commonwealthfund.org/publications/fund-reports/2024/sep/mirror-mirror-2024

68 Noam Levey, "Some Hospitals Rake in High Profits While Their Patients Are Loaded with Medical Debt," *NPR,* 28 September 2022, https://www.npr.org/sections/

health-shots/2022/09/28/1125176699/some-hospitals-rake-in-high-profits-while-their-patients-are-loaded-with-medical

69   See https://pages.stern.nyu.edu/~adamodar/New_Home_Page/datafile/margin.html

70   Carol Davis, "Most U.S. Nonprofit Hospitals Neglect Community Investment Obligation," *Health Leaders Media*, 9 July 2021, https://www.healthleadersmedia.com/clinical-care/most-us-nonprofit-hospitals-neglect-community-investment-obligation

71   World Health Organization, "World Health Organization Assesses the World's Health Systems," 7 February 2000, https://www.who.int/news/item/07-02-2000-world-health-organization-assesses-the-world's-health-systems; see also Lydia Saad, "Americans Sour on U.S. Healthcare Quality," *Gallup News*, 19 January 2023, https://news.gallup.com/poll/468176/americans-sour-healthcare-quality.aspx

72   Munira Z. Gunja, Evan D. Dumas, and Reginald D. Williams II, "The U.S. Maternal Mortality Crisis Continues to Worsen: An International Comparison," *Commonwealth Fund*, 1 December 2022, https://www.commonwealthfund.org/blog/2022/us-maternal-mortality-crisis-continues-worsen-international-comparison; see also https://www.cdc.gov/maternal-infant-health/infant-mortality/index.html; https://www.oecd.org/en/data/indicators/infant-mortality-rates.html

73   Rabah Kamal and Julie Hudman, "What Do We Know About Spending Related to Public Health in the U.S. and Comparable Countries?" *Peterson-KFF Health System Tracker*, 30 September 2020, https://www.oecd.org/en/data/indicators/infant-mortality-rates.html

74   Pensions & Investments, "The Largest Foundations," 21 November 2018, https://www.pionline.com/article/20181112/ONLINE/181109876/the-largest-foundations; see also https://www.influencewatch.org/for-profit/chan-zuckerberg-initiative

75   Merianne R. Spencer, Holly Hedegaard, and Margaret Warner,

"Unintentional Drowning Deaths Among Children Aged 0–17 Years: United States, 1999–2019," National Center for Health Statistics Data Brief No. 413, July 2021, https://www.cdc.gov/nchs/products/databriefs/db413.htm; see also https://report.nih.gov/funding/categorical-spending; https://www.cdc.gov/vitalsigns/drowning/index.html

76   World Health Organization, *Global Report On Drowning: Preventing A Leading Killer* (2014), https://www.who.int/publications/i/item/global-report-on-drowning-preventing-a-leading-killer; World Health Organization, *Preventing Drowning: An Implementation Guide* (2017), https://www.who.int/publications/i/item/preventing-drowning-an-implementation-guide; Aminur Rahman, Lamisa Ashram, Akm F. Rahman et al., "Retention of Survival Swimming Skills Among SwimSafe Graduates in Rural Communities of Bangladesh: Results from a Cross-Sectional Study," *Injury Prevention*. Epub 26 July 2024. doi: 10.1136/ip-2024-045309, https://pubmed.ncbi.nlm.nih.gov/39060116/

77   Bloomberg Philanthropies, "Bloomberg Philanthropies Invests Additional $60 Million to Help Prevent Drowning Deaths Globally," press release, 14 May 2024, https://www.bloomberg.org/press/bloomberg-philanthropies-invests-additional-60-million-to-help-prevent-drowning-deaths-globally

78   Michael Jacobson, "Swim Study Reveals a Smart Pool of Talent," *Griffith University*, 13 August 2013, https://news.griffith.edu.au/2013/08/13/swimming-a-smart-move-for-children/

79   See https://wisqars.cdc.gov/cost

80   National Drowning Prevention Alliance, "The Latest Drowning Statistics," n.d., https://ndpa.org/parenttoolkit//BlogsParentToolkit/BLOG-The Latest Drowning Statistics-NDPA.pdf

81   Australian Water Safety Council, *Australian Water Safety Strategy 2030* (2021), https://doi.org/10.62977/TPLX4043

82   Drowning Prevention Research Centre, *Canadian Drowning*

Prevention Plan, 9th edn (Fredericton, NB: DPRC/Canadian Drowning Prevention Coalition, 2022), https://www.lifesavingsociety.com/media/370340/cdndrowningpreventionplan-en-9thedition-20220520.pdf; National Water Safety Forum, *A Future Without Drowning: The UK Drowning Prevention Strategy 2016–2026.* (2015), https://www.nationalwatersafety.org.uk/strategy/; Water Safety New Zealand, *Drowning Prevention Report 2023* (2023), https://www.watersafetynz.org/_files/ugd/6f2a10_9ec6a70c05b84703bc2c45a491da163f.pdf

83   See https://www.watersafetyusa.org

84   World Health Organization, *Preventing Drowning: An Implementation Guide* (2017), https://www.who.int/publications/i/item/9789241511933; USNWSAP, *U.S. National Water Safety Action Plan 2023–2032* (2023), https://www.watersafetyusa.org/nwsap.html

85   United Nations, *The Sustainable Development Goals Report 2023: Special Edition* (New York: UN DESA, 2023), https://unstats.un.org/sdgs/report/2023/

86   Pooja Bhadoria, Gaurisha Gupta, and Anubha Agarwal, "Viral Pandemics in the Past Two Decades: An Overview," *Journal of Family Medicine and Primary Care.* 2021. 10(8): 2745–2750, https://journals.lww.com/jfmpc/Fulltext/2021/10080/Viral_Pandemics_in_the_Past_Two_Decades__An.5.aspx?

87   Hseuh-Fen Chen and Salema A. Karim, "Relationship Between Political Partisanship and COVID-19 Deaths: Future Implications for Public Health," *Journal of Public Health (Oxford).* 2022. 44(3): 716–723. doi: 10.1093/pubmed/fdab136

CHAPTER 4

88   Arthur Conan Doyle, "The Adventures of the Copper Beeches," *Arthur Conan Doyle Encyclopedia*, https://www.arthur-conan-doyle.com/search-fictions/?n=COPP&v=195#195

89   "Data," *Merriam-Webster Dictionary*, https://www.

merriam-webster.com/dictionary/data

90   Forbes Wealth Team, "America's Top Givers 2022: The 25 Most Philanthropic Billionaires," *Forbes*, 6 May 2022, https://www.forbes.com/sites/forbeswealthteam/2022/01/19/americas-top-givers-2022-the-25-most-philanthropic-billionaires/

91   Mike Bloomberg, "You Can't Manage What You Can't Measure," *LinkedIn*, 10 January 2020, https://www.linkedin.com/pulse/you-cant-manage-what-measure-mike-bloomberg/

92   Ronald H. Coase, *How Should Economists Choose? The G. Warren Nutter Lectures in Political Economy* (Washington, DC: American Enterprise Institute, 1982), p. 16, https://www.aei.org/wp-content/uploads/2016/03/NutterLectures03.pdf?x85095

93   Daniel Kahneman and Amos Tversky, "Prospect Theory: An Analysis of Decision Under Risk," *Econometrica*. 1979. 47(2): 263–292, https://www.jstor.org/stable/1914185

94   Seo Myeong-Gu Seo and Lisa F. Barrett, "Being Emotional During Decision Making – Good or Bad? An Empirical Investigation," *Academy of Management Journal*. 2007. 50(4): 923–940. doi: 10.5465/amj.2007.26279217, https://www.ncbi.nlm.nih.gov/pmc/articles/PMC2361392/

95   The Economist, "Rethinking Thinking," 16 December 1999, https://www.economist.com/christmas-specials/1999/12/16/rethinking-thinking

96   Ronald L. Wasserstein, "A Statistician's View: What Are Your Chances of Winning the Powerball Lottery?" *Huffington Post*, 16 March 2013 (updated 6 December 2017), https://www.huffpost.com/entry/chances-of-winning-powerball-lottery_b_3288129; Robert Gebeloff, Danielle Ivory, Bill Marsh, Allison McCann, and Albert Sun, "Childhood's Greatest Danger: The Data on Kids and Gun Violence," *New York Times*, 14 December 2014, https://www.nytimes.com/interactive/2022/12/14/magazine/gun-violence-children-data-statistics.html; Rebecca M. Cunningham, Maureen A. Walton, and Patrick M. Carter, "The Major Causes of Death

in Children and Adolescents in the United States," *New England Journal of Medicine*. 2018. 379(25): 2468–2475, https://www.nejm.org/doi/full/10.1056/NEJMsr1804754; U.S. Government Accountability Office, "The Rising Threat of Domestic Terrorism in the U.S. and Federal Efforts to Combat It," 2 March 2023, https://www.gao.gov/blog/rising-threat-domestic-terrorism-u.s.-and-federal-efforts-combat-it; World Health Organization, "Road Traffic Injuries," 13 December 2023, https://www.who.int/en/news-room/fact-sheets/detail/road-traffic-injuries; https://injuryfacts.nsc.org/all-injuries/preventable-death-overview/odds-of-dying/

97   Edward Luce, "Beware Elon Musk's Warped Libertarianism," *Financial Times*, 24 May 2023, https://www.ft.com/content/7ca8e38d-8ecf-4de2-870d-9bd0a2476147

98   See https://aynrand.org/novels/the-virtue-of-selfishness; see also Denise Cummins, "This Is What Happens When You Take Ayn Rand Seriously," *PBS News*, 16 February 2016, https://www.pbs.org/newshour/economy/column-this-is-what-happens-when-you-take-ayn-rand-seriously; Rutger Bregman, *Humankind: A Hopeful History* (London: Little, Brown and Company, 2019).

99   Peter Thiel, "Education of a Libertarian," *CATO Unbound: A Journal of Debate*, 13 April 2009, https://www.cato-unbound.org/2009/04/13/peter-thiel/education-libertarian/

100 Sarah Myers West, Meredith Whittaker, and Kate Crawford, "Discriminating Systems: Gender, Race and Power in AI," *AI Now Institute*, April 2019, https://ainowinstitute.org/publication/discriminating-systems-gender-race-and-power-in-ai-2

101 Kate Crawford, Roel Dobbe, Theodora Dryer, Genevieve Fried, Ben Green, Elizabeth Kaziunas, et al., *AI Now 2019 Report* (New York: AI Now Institute, 2019), https://ainowinstitute.org/publication/ai-now-2019-report-2

102 Lama H. Nazer, Razan Zatarah, Shai Waldrip, Janny X. C. Ke, Mira Moukheiber, Ashish Khanna et al., "Bias in Artificial Intelligence Algorithms and Recommendations for Mitigation,"

PLOS Digital Health. 2023. 22(6): e0000278. doi: 10.1371/journal.pdig.0000278, https://www.ncbi.nlm.nih.gov/pmc/articles/PMC10287014/; Aniya Greene-Santos, "Does AI Have a Bias Problem?" *NEA Today,* 22 February 2024, https://www.nea.org/nea-today/all-news-articles/does-ai-have-bias-problem

103   James Manyika, Jake Silberg, and Brittany Presten, "What Do We Do About the Biases in AI?" *Harvard Business Review,* 25 October 2019, https://hbr.org/2019/10/what-do-we-do-about-the-biases-in-ai

104   Einar H. Dyvik, "Leading Industries Worldwide 2019–2023, By Revenue," *Statista,* 7 August 2024, https://www.statista.com/statistics/264730/the-top-20-most-profitable-branches-of-industry-worldwide/

105   Investopedia Team, "Which Industry Spends the Most on Lobbying?" *Investopedia,* updated 19 February 2024, https://www.investopedia.com/investing/which-industry-spends-most-lobbying-antm-so/

106   Paul Kiel and Jesse Eisinger, "How the IRS was Gutted," *ProPublica,* 11 December 2018, https://www.propublica.org/article/how-the-irs-was-gutted; Vanessa Williamson, "Cutting IRS Funding is a Gift to America's Wealthiest Tax Evaders," *Brookings Institution,* 26 June 2023, https://www.brookings.edu/articles/cutting-irs-funding-is-a-gift-to-americas-wealthiest-tax-evaders/

107   Brandi Buchman, "Budget Cuts Cripple EPA Enforcement as Cases and Investigations Plummet," *Courthouse News Service,* 28 August 2017, https://www.courthousenews.com/budget-cuts-cripple-epa-enforcement-public-interest-group-says/

108   Aldous Huxley, *Proper Studies* (London: Chatto and Windus, 1929), p. 221.

109   See https://www.impact.upenn.edu/early-childhood-toolkit/why-invest/what-is-the-return-on-investment

110   Sarah A. Denny, Linda Quan, Julie Gilchrist, Tracy McCallin, Rohit Shenoi, Shabana Yusuf, et al., "Prevention of Drowning," *Pediatrics.* 2019. 143(5): e20190850, https://doi.org/10.1542/peds.2019-0850

111   Fazlur Rahman, Saideep Bose, Michael Linnan, Aminur Rahman, Saidur Mashreky, Benjamin Haaland, and Eric Finkelstein, "Cost-effectiveness of an Injury and Drowning Prevention Program in Bangladesh," *Pediatrics.* 2012. 130(6): e1621-8. doi: 10.1542/peds.2012-0757, https://pubmed.ncbi.nlm.nih.gov/23147971/

112   See https://www.safekids.org/sites/default/files/documents/drowning-fast-facts.pdf

113   Tracy E. McCallin, Mickenzie Morgan, Margaret L.I. Hart, and Shabana Yusuf, "Epidemiology, Prevention, and Sequelae of Drowning," *Pediatrics in Review.* 2021. 42(3): 123–132, https://pubmed.ncbi.nlm.nih.gov/33648991/

114   Michael Linnan, Aminur Rahman, Justin Scarr, Tracie Reinten-Reynolds, Huan Linnan, Jing Rui-wei et al., *Child Drowning: Evidence for a Newly Recognized Cause of Child Mortality in Low and Middle Income Countries in Asia.* Special Series on Child Injury, Working Paper 2012-07 (Florence: UNICEF Office of Research, 2012), https://archive.crin.org/en/docs/drowning.pdf

115   Samuel P. Hills, Matthew Hobbs, Michael J. Tipton, and Martin J. Barwood, "The Water Incident Database (WAID) 2012 to 2019: A Systematic Evaluation of the Documenting of UK Drownings," *BMC Public Health.* 2021. 21: 1760, https://doi.org/10.1186/s12889-021-11827-0, https://bmcpublichealth.biomedcentral.com/articles/10.1186/s12889-021-11827-0; see also https://www.royallifesaving.com.au/research-and-policy/drowning-research/summer-drowning-toll

116   Puspa Raj Pant, "Fatal Drownings in Nepal: As Reported in the Media," presentation at the World Conference on Drowning Prevention, Danang, Vietnam, 10–13 May 2011, https://www.researchgate.net/publication/247773884_Fatal_drownings_in_nepal_as_reported_in_the_media; Mable Nakitto, Bonnie Wandera, and Ronald Lett, "Drowning in the Great Lakes of Uganda: A Neglected Problem," *Injury Prevention.* 2012. 180: A132–A133, https://injuryprevention.bmj.com/content/18/

Suppl_1/A132.4

CHAPTER 5

117 Chip Heath and Dan Heath, *Made to Stick: Why Some Ideas Survive and Others Die* (London: Random House, 2007).

118 William H. George, Kelly C. Davis, N. Tatiana Masters, Kelly F. Kajumulo, Cynthia A. Stappenbeck, Jeanette Norris et al., "Partner Pressure, Victimization History, and Alcohol: Women's Condom-Decision Abdication Mediated by Mood and Anticipated Negative Partner Reaction," *AIDS and Behavior.* 2016. 20 Suppl 1(01): S134–146. doi: 10.1007/s10461-015-1154-3, https://www.ncbi.nlm.nih.gov/pmc/articles/PMC4758682/; Casey E. Copen, "Condom Use During Sexual Intercourse Among Women and Men Aged 15–44 in the United States: 2011–2015 National Survey of Family Growth," National Health Statistics Reports, No. 105, 10 August 2017, https://www.cdc.gov/nchs/data/nhsr/nhsr105.pdf; see also https://data.worldbank.org/indicator/SH.CON.1524.MA.ZS

119 World Health Organization, "Alarming Decline in Adolescent Condom Use, Increased Risk of Sexually Transmitted Infections and Unintended Pregnancies, Reveals New WHO Report," 29 August 2024, https://www.who.int/europe/news/item/29-08-2024-alarming-decline-in-adolescent-condom-use--increased-risk-of-sexually-transmitted-infections-and-unintended-pregnancies--reveals-new-who-report

120 Michael Linnan, Aminur Rahman, Justin Scarr, Tracie Reinten-Reynolds, Huan Linnan, Jing Rui-wei, et al., *Child Drowning: Evidence for a Newly Recognized Cause of Child Mortality in Low and Middle Income Countries in Asia,* Special Series on Child Injury, Working Paper 2012-07 (Florence: UNICEF Office of Research, 2012), https://archive.crin.org/en/docs/drowning.pdf

121 David A. Larsen, Joseph Makaure, Sadie J. Ryan, Donald Stewart, Adrianne Traub, Rick Welsh et al., "Implications of Insecticide-Treated Mosquito Net Fishing in Lower Income Countries,"

Environmental Health Perspectives. 2021. 129(1): 15001. doi: 10.1289/EHP7001, https://ehp.niehs.nih.gov/doi/10.1289/EHP7001

122 Surf Without Borders presentation, World Conference on Drowning Prevention, Danang, Vietnam, 10–13 May 2011; see also https://www.surfwithoutborders.org/

123 Purbita Saha, "The Real Story Behind the War Against DDT," *Audubon*. 24 July 2015, https://www.audubon.org/news/the-real-story-behind-war-against-ddt; Mike Magner, "House Readies to Help Bald Eagle Soar as National Bird," *Roll Call*, 3 September 2024, https://rollcall.com/2024/09/03/house-readies-to-help-bald-eagle-soar-as-national-bird/; see also https://www.philippineeaglefoundation.org/philippine-eagle

124 Shreya Dasgupta, "Saudi Prince Kills Two Percent of Global Population of Endangered Bird," *Mongabay*, 1 May 2014, https://news.mongabay.com/2014/05/saudi-prince-kills-two-percent-of-global-population-of-endangered-bird/; Mary Bowerman, "Minnesota Dentist 'Deeply' Regrets 'Taking' Cecil the Lion," *USA Today*, 28 July 2015, https://www.usatoday.com/story/news/nation-now/2015/07/28/minnesota-dentist-walter-james-palmer-cecil-lion-africa/30785881/; Yang Siqi, "The Chinese Elite's New Love of Hunting Has Conservationists Worried," *Time Magazine*, 15 April 2016, https://time.com/4295534/china-hunting-wildlife-endangered/; Paula Froelich, "Cecil the Lion's Killer is Back – Slaughtering Endangered Rams in Mongolia," *New York Post*, 11 July 2020, https://nypost.com/2020/07/11/cecil-the-lions-killer-slaughters-endangered-mongolian-ram/

125 Casie H. Morgan, "Your Friendly Neighborhood Superkid: The Influence of Superheroes on Children's Risk-Taking Behaviors" (2020), unpublished thesis, University of Alabama at Birmingham, https://digitalcommons.library.uab.edu/etd-collection/2515/

126 See https://www.youtube.com/watch?v=QOlXkeRVpY0

127 See https://www.youtube.com/watch?v=2_tIs1sk8OY

128   See https://www.youtube.com/watch?v=YrLk4vdY28Q

129   Shahram Heshmat, "Music, Emotion, and Well-Being: How Does Music Affect the Way We Think, Feel, and Behave?" *Psychology Today*, 25 August 2019, https://www.psychologytoday.com/us/blog/science-choice/201908/music-emotion-and-well-being

130   See https://www.ilsf.org/international-open-water-drowning-prevention-guidelines/

CHAPTER 6

131   Modern translation. The earlier translation reads, "For as man is the best of the animals when perfected, so he is the worst of all when sundered from law and justice": Aristotle, *Aristotle in 23 Volumes*, Vol. 21, tr. H. Rackham. (Cambridge, MA: Harvard University Press; London: William Heinemann, 1944), https://www.perseus.tufts.edu/hopper/text?doc=Perseus:text:1999.01.0058:book=1:section=1253a

132   Christina Acuna and Reagan Bleasdell, "64. Thomas More: Utopia," *An Open Companion to Early British Literature*, 2019, https://pressbooks.pub/earlybritishlit/chapter/sir-thomas-more-utopia/

133   See https://thealaskafrontier.com/weird-laws-in-alaska; https://legislature.idaho.gov/statutesrules/idstat/title18/t18ch50/sect18-5003/

134   Adolfo Flores and Jennifer Calfas, "States Look to Ease Some Child-Labor Laws Amid Tight Market," *Wall Street Journal*, 10 March 2023, https://www.wsj.com/articles/states-look-to-ease-some-child-labor-laws-amid-tight-market-a46322c6; Christopher J. Brooks, "Iowa Moves to Weaken Child Labor Laws, Joining Other States," *CBS News*, 4 May 2023, https://www.cbsnews.com/news/iowa-child-labor-law-hours-teens/

135   See https://www.ohchr.org/en/instruments-mechanisms/instruments/convention-rights-child

136   Cindy Wooden, "Pope Decides Women Will Be Voting Members of Synod of Bishops," *United States Conference of Catholic*

Bishops, 26 April 2023, https://www.usccb.org/news/2023/pope-decides-women-will-be-voting-members-synod-bishops

137 Max Boot, *Invisible Armies: An Epic History of Guerrilla Warfare from Ancient Times to the Present* (New York and London: Liveright Publishing, 2013).

138 Damon Centola, Joshua Becker, Devon Brackbill, and Andrea Baronchelli, "Experimental Evidence for Tipping Points in Social Convention," *Science*. 2018. 360(6393): 1116–1119, https://www.science.org/doi/10.1126/science.aas8827; Julie Sloane, "Research Finds Tipping Point for Large-Scale Social Change," *Annenberg School of Communication, University of Pennsylvania*, 7 June 2018, https://www.asc.upenn.edu/news-events/news/research-finds-tipping-point-large-scale-social-change

139 Thomas P. Slaughter, *Independence: The Tangled Roots of the American Revolution* (New York: Hill and Wang, 2014). Summary of book: Rachel Goldstein, "Three Things You Didn't Know About the American Revolution," *University of Rochester*, 1 July 2016, https://www.rochester.edu/newscenter/three-things-you-didnt-know-about-the-american-revolution/

140 See https://history.state.gov/milestones/1776-1783/french-alliance

141 Kevin Bales, *New Slavery: A Reference Handbook*, 2nd edn (Santa Barbara, CA: ABC-CLIO, 2004), pp. 55–68; Richard Hellie, "Slavery." *Encyclopedia Britannica*, 16 September 2024, https://www.britannica.com/topic/slavery-sociology; see also https://www.archives.gov/milestone-documents/13th-amendment

142 Manuel Velasquez, Claire Andre, Thomas Shanks, S. J., and Michael J. Meyer, "Ethical Relativism," *Santa Clara University*, 1 August 1992, https://www.scu.edu/ethics/ethics-resources/ethical-decision-making/ethical-relativism/

143 Grant Ennis, *How PR and the Fog of Corporate Disinformation Has Governments Paying to Burn the Planet* (Cantley, QC: Daraja Press, 2023).

144 Jamie Freestone, "To Get Conservative Climate Contrarians to

Really Listen, Try Speaking Their Language," *The Conversation*, 15 May 2018, https://theconversation.com/to-get-conservative-climate-contrarians-to-really-listen-try-speaking-their-language-94296

145 Illinois Secretary of State, "Illinois GDL Parent-Teen Driving Guide Graduated Driver Licensing Program," July 2023, https://www.ilsos.gov/publications/pdf_publications/dsd_a217.pdf

146 See https://www.youtube.com/watch?v=mr4aFTFHW3A

147 See https://swimfin.co.uk

148 See https://lifestraw.com/collections/straw-filters

149 See https://www.youtube.com/watch?v=hPXjzsXJ1Y0

150 See https://oceanjunction.com/collections/swim-buddy

151 Casey W. Pirnstill and Gerard L. Coté, "Malaria Diagnosis Using a Mobile Phone Polarized Microscope," *Scientific Reports*. 2015. 25(5): 13368. doi: 10.1038/srep13368, https://www.ncbi.nlm.nih.gov/pmc/articles/PMC4548194/; Donald G. McNeil Jr., "In African Villages, These Phones Become Ultrasound Scanners: A Hand-Held Device Brings Medical Imaging to Remote Communities, Often for the First Time," *New York Times*, 15 April 2019, https://www.nytimes.com/2019/04/15/health/medical-scans-butterfly-iq.html

152 Swim Vietnam presentation, World Conference on Drowning Prevention, Danang, Vietnam, 10–13 May 2011.

153 See https://esgthereport.com/what-is-social-washing/

154 Bertrand Hauger, "Floating Backpacks to Save Kids' Lives in Vietnam," WorldCrunch, 3 December 2012, https://worldcrunch.com/tech-science/floating-backpacks-to-save-kids039-lives-in-vietnam; Kyle Bakx, "Oil, Politics and Human Rights: A Look Back at Talisman," CBC News, 22 February 2015, https://www.cbc.ca/news/business/oil-politics-and-human-rights-a-look-back-at-talisman-1.2964715

155 Steve Schering, "Practice Water Safety to Prepare for Summer Fun," *American Academy of Pediatrics*, 1 June

2024, https://publications.aap.org/aapnews/news/28849/ Practice-water-safety-to-prepare-for-summer-fun

156   "Did Coca-Cola Ever Contain Cocaine?" *Just Think Twice*, n.d., https://www.justthinktwice.gov/article/ did-coca-cola-ever-contain-cocaine

157   T. E. C. Jr., "What Were Godfrey's Cordial and Dalby's Carminative?" *Pediatrics*. 1970. 45(6): 1011, https://publications. aap.org/pediatrics/article-abstract/45/6/1011/78158/ WHAT-WERE-GODFREY-S-CORDIAL-AND-DALBY- S?redirectedFrom=fulltext

158   Lucy Ravenhall, "How to Recycle Summer's Pool Inflatables," *Forge Recycling UK*, 27 September 2019, https://www.forgerecycling. co.uk/blog/how-to-recycle-summers-pool-inflatables/

159   Mike Muller, "The Baby Killer: A War on Want Investigation into the Promotion and Sale of Powdered Baby Milks in the Third World," *War on Want*, March 1974, http://archive.babymilkaction. org/pdfs/babykiller.pdf

160   Leslie Shaffer, "Nestlé Chairman: Time to Turn Off the Water Taps," *CNBC*, 24 March 2015, https://www.cnbc. com/2015/03/24/nestle-chairman-time-to-turn-off-the-water- taps.html; Arthur Neslen, "Nestlé Under Fire for Marketing Claims on Baby Milk Formulas," *The Guardian*, 1 February 2018, https://www.theguardian.com/business/2018/feb/01/ nestle-under-fire-for-marketing-claims-on-baby-milk-formulas

161   Marc Gunther, "Under Pressure: Campaigns That Persuaded Companies to Change the World," *Campaign for Safe Cosmetics*, 9 February 2015, https://www.safecosmetics.org/blog/under- pressure-campaigns-that-persuaded-companies-to-change-the- world/

162   Business Wire, "Asia Pulp and Paper Signs New York Declaration on Forests at UN Climate Summit to Help Tackle Climate Change," 23 September 2014, https:// www.businesswire.com/news/home/20140923006133/en/

Asia-Pulp-and-Paper-signs-New-York-Declaration-on-Forests-at-UN-Climate-Summit-to-help-tackle-climate-change

163 Matt Wiley and Scott Lichtig, "The Nike Controversy," *Stanford University*, n.d., https://web.stanford.edu/class/e297c/trade_environment/wheeling/hnike.html; https://about.nike.com/en/impact-resources/statement-on-forced-labor

164 See https://www.youtube.com/watch?v=EM3g-uW592k

165 Penelope A. Phillips-Howard, Elizabeth Nyothach, Feiko Oter Kuile, Jackton Omoto, Duolao Wang, Clement Zeh et al., "Menstrual Cups and Sanitary Pads to Reduce School Attrition, and Sexually Transmitted and Reproductive Tract Infections: A Cluster Randomised Controlled Feasibility Study in Rural Western Kenya," *BMJ Open*. 2016. 6: e013229. doi: 10.1136/bmjopen-2016-013229, https://bmjopen.bmj.com/content/6/11/e013229; Garazi Zulaika, Elizabeth Nyothach, Anna Maria van Eijk, Duolao Wang, Valarie Opollo, David Obor et al., "Menstrual Cups and Cash Transfer to Reduce Sexual and Reproductive Harm and School Dropout in Adolescent Schoolgirls in Western Kenya: A Cluster Randomised Controlled Trial," *eClinicalMedicine*. 2023. 10(65):102261. doi: 10.1016/j.eclinm.2023.102261, https://www.ncbi.nlm.nih.gov/pmc/articles/PMC10582356/

166 Alex Taylor III, "Harley-Davidson's Aging Biker Problem," *CNN Money*, 17 September 2010, https://money.cnn.com/2010/09/17/autos/harley_davidson_fall.fortune/index.htm

167 Reuters, "Black South Africans Still Earn Far Less Than Whites – Survey," 27 January 2017, https://www.reuters.com/article/world/black-south-africans-still-earn-far-less-than-whites-survey-idUSKBN15B173/

168 See https://www.britannica.com/list/nelson-mandela-quotes

CHAPTER 7

169 John Maynard Keynes, *The General Theory of Employment, Interest and Money*, ch. 21: The Theory of Prices, Section I, https://www.

marxists.org/reference/subject/economics/keynes/general-theory/ch21.htm

170   Ian Altman, "Half of Nonprofits Are Set Up to Fail – How About Your Favorite," *Forbes*, 21 March 2016, https://www.forbes.com/sites/ianaltman/2016/03/20/half-of-nonprofits-are-setup-to-fail-how-about-your-favorite/

171   Michael T. Deane, "Top 6 Reasons New Businesses Fail," *Investopedia*, 1 June 2024, https://www.investopedia.com/financial-edge/1010/top-6-reasons-new-businesses-fail.aspx

172   Greg McRay, "Top 5 Reasons Why Nonprofits Fail," *Foundation Group*, 28 May 2024, https://www.501c3.org/top-5-reasons-why-nonprofits-fail/

173   Michael Bradley, "Luxurious and Lavish: Why a Bugatti Will Cost You Several Million," *Luxe Digital*, updated 29 April 2024, https://luxe.digital/lifestyle/garage/bugatti-price-list/

174   Jeff Perez, "20 Cheapest Cars, Trucks, and SUVs in the US for 2023," *Motor1*, 13 January 2023, https://www.motor1.com/features/631073/cheapest-cars-trucks-suvs-2023/

175   Albert Camus, *Carnets, 1935–1942*, tr. Philip Thody (London: Hamish Hamilton, 1963), p. 43, https://archive.org/details/carnets193519420000albe

176   ESPN, "Highest-Paid NFL players: Most Guaranteed Money at Every Position," 8 September 2024, https://www.espn.com/nfl/story/_/id/34096853/highest-paid-nfl-players-tracking-most-money-guaranteed-per-year-every-positionz; https://www.salary.com/research/salary/benchmark/public-school-teacher-salary; U.S. Department of Labor, Bureau of Labor Statistics, "Usual Weekly Earnings of Age and Salary Workers Second Quarter 2024," News Release USDL-24-1410, 17 July 2024, https://www.bls.gov/news.release/pdf/wkyeng.pdf

177   Raj Chetty, John N. Friedman, and Jonah E. Rockoff. "Measuring the Impacts of Teachers I: Evaluating Bias in Teacher Value-Added Estimates," *American Economic Review*. 2014. 104(9):

2593–2632. doi: 10.1257/aer.104.9.2593, https://www.aeaweb.org/articles?id=10.1257/aer.104.9.2593; Raj Chetty, John N. Friedman, and Jonah E. Rockoff, "Measuring the Impacts of Teachers II: Teacher Value-Added and Student Outcomes in Adulthood," *American Economic Review*. 2014. 104 (9): 2633–79. doi: 10.1257/aer.104.9.2633, https://www.aeaweb.org/articles?id=10.1257/aer.104.9.2633

178 Christina Gough, "Total Revenue of the NFL 2001–2022," *Statista*, 5 September 2022, https://www.statista.com/statistics/193457/total-league-revenue-of-the-nfl-since-2005/; Ken Belson, "How Roger Goodell Became the NFL's $20 Billion Man," *New York Times*, 12 October 2024; see also https://www.irs.gov/charities-non-profits/other-non-profits/professional-football-leagues

179 National Nurses United, "Nurses Named Most Trusted Profession for 22nd Consecutive Year," 22 January 2024, https://www.nationalnursesunited.org/press/nurses-named-most-trusted-profession-22nd-consecutive-year; see also https://www.bls.gov/oes/current/oes291141.htm

180 Frank Bass and Rita Beamish, "$1.6B of Bank Bailout Went to Execs," *CBS News*, 21 December 2008, https://www.cbsnews.com/news/16b-of-bank-bailout-went-to-execs/

181 Lawrence Mishel and Jori Kandra, "CEO Pay Has Skyrocketed 1,322% Since 1978: CEOs Were Paid 351 Times as Much as a Typical Worker in 2020," *Economic Policy Institute*, 10 August 2021, https://www.epi.org/publication/ceo-pay-in-2020/

182 Drew Desilver, "For Most U.S. Workers, Real Wages Have Barely Budged in Decades," *Pew Research Center,* 7 August 2018, https://www.pewresearch.org/short-reads/2018/08/07/for-most-us-workers-real-wages-have-barely-budged-for-decades/

183 See https://www.youtube.com/watch?v=VVxYOQS6ggk; see also John Paul Rollert, "The Moral Ambivalence of Gordon Gekko," *Chicago Booth Review*, 18 August 2017, https://www.chicagobooth.edu/review/moral-ambivalence-gordon-gekko

184 Josh Givens and Jori Kandra, "CEO Pay Has Skyrocketed 1,460% Since 1978," *Economic Policy Institute*, 4 October 2022, https://www.epi.org/publication/ceo-pay-in-2021/; See https://www.charitywatch.org/nonprofit-compensation-packages-of-1-million-or-more

185 Al Mueller, "2021–2022 Nonprofit CEO Compensation Study," *Excellence in Giving*, 22 August 2022, https://analytics.excellenceingiving.com/2021-2022-nonprofit-ceo-compensation-study/

186 Mehdi Punjwani, Bryce Colburn, and Sierra Campbell, "Average Salary in the U.S. in 2024," updated 3 April 2024, https://www.usatoday.com/money/blueprint/business/hr-payroll/average-salary-us/; see also https://npcrowd.com/nonprofit-employee-pay

187 VGG Communications, "Social Interventions and What You Need to Know About Them," *Medium*, 4 October 2019, https://communications-25371.medium.com/social-interventions-and-what-you-need-to-know-about-them-cdbf2c3a37a

188 Mark R. Leary and Shira Gabriel, "The Relentless Pursuit of Acceptance and Belonging." In Andrew J. Elliot (ed.), *Advances in Motivation Science, Volume 9* (Cambridge, MA: Academic Press, 2022), pp. 135–178.

189 Tina M. Olsson, Sabina Kapetanovic, Katarina Hollertz, Mikaela Starke, and Therése Skoog, "Advancing Social Intervention Research Through Program Theory Reconstruction," *Research on Social Work Practice*. 2023. 33(6), https://journals.sagepub.com/doi/full/10.1177/10497315221149976#bibr62-10497315221149976

190 See https://www.sbcguidance.org/do/social-norms

191 Adam Eckert, "Billionaire Warren Buffett Still Lives in an Old Corner House He Purchased for $32K," *Yahoo Finance,* 2 October 2024, https://finance.yahoo.com/news/billionaire-warren-buffett-still-lives-001947793.html

192 Chris Stevenson, "Paul Allen: Superyachts, Sports Teams, Warplanes and a Jimi Hendrix Museum – The Many Loves of

Microsoft's 'Idea Man,'" *The Independent*, 17 October 2018, https://www.independent.co.uk/news/world/americas/paul-allen-death-reclusive-yacht-bill-gates-microsoft-seattle-seahawks-a8585621.html

193   Emily A. Shrider, Melissa Dollar, Frances Chen, Jessica Semega, *Income and Poverty in the United States: 2020*. Report Number P60-273. United States Census Bureau, 14 September 2021, https://www.census.gov/library/publications/2021/demo/p60-273.html; Forbes, "The Real-Time Billionaires List," 2024, https://www.forbes.com/real-time-billionaires/#177f661c3d78

194   See https://www.youtube.com/watch?v=vuLwjFmESrg

195   Heinrich Himmler, "Excerpt from Himler's Speech to the SS-Gruppenführer at Posen (October 4, 1942)," *German History in Documents and Images*, https://ghdi.ghi-dc.org/sub_document.cfm?document_id=1513

CHAPTER 8

196   Edmund Burke, "Letter I: On the Overtures of Peace." *Two Letters Addressed to a Member of the Present Parliament, on the Proposals for Peace with the Regicide Directory of France* (London: F. and C. Rivington, 1790), https://quod.lib.umich.edu/cgi/t/text/text-idx?c=ecco;idno=004904033.0001.000

197   United States: see https://fiscaldata.treasury.gov/americas-finance-guide/federal-spending

198   China: see Brian Hart, Bonny Lin, Matthew P. Funaiole, Samantha Lu, Hannah Price, and Matthew Slade, "Making Sense of China's Government Budget," *China Power*, 15 March 2023 (updated 14 March 2024), https://chinapower.csis.org/making-sense-of-chinas-government-budget/

199   Baltimore: see Brandon M. Scott, *Fiscal 2023: Summary of the Adopted Budget* (Baltimore, MD: Department of Finance, City of Baltimore, 2022), https://bbmr.baltimorecity.gov/sites/default/files/FY23_SOTA_final_Update.pdf

200 Chicago: see https://www.chicago.gov/content/dam/city/depts/
     obm/supp_info/2023Budget/2023BudgetInfographic.pdf

201 See https://www.cancer.org/research/currently-funded-cancer-
     research/grants-by-cancer-type.html

202 See https://www.youtube.com/watch?v=vuLwjFmESrg

203 Baltimore was presented with the Government Finance Officers
     Association's Distinguished Budget Presentation Award for the
     fiscal year beginning 1 July 202. See City of Baltimore, Maryland,
     Fiscal 2023: Summary of the Adopted Budget (2023), p. iii, https://
     bbmr.baltimorecity.gov/sites/default/files/FY23_SOTA_final_
     Update.pdf

204 See https://ceo.lacounty.gov/budget

205 See https://council.nyc.gov/budget; see also State of New York
     Comptroller, *Review of the Financial Plan of the City of New York.
     Report 16-2022* (2021), https://www.osc.ny.gov/files/reports/osdc/
     pdf/report-16-2022.pdf

206 City of Chicago, 2024 Budget Review (2024), https://www.chicago.
     gov/content/dam/city/depts/obm/supp_info/2024Budget/2024-
     Budget-Overview_CityofChicago.pdf

207 See https://www.coca-colacompany.com/about-us/history/
     new-coke-the-most-memorable-marketing-blunder-ever

208 Jeff Turrentine, "What Are the Causes of Climate Change?"
     Natural Resource Defense Council, 13 September 2022, https://
     www.nrdc.org/stories/what-are-causes-climate-change#human;
     see also https://science.nasa.gov/climate-change/faq/
     do-scientists-agree-on-climate-change/

209 Alice Fabbri, Alexandra Lai, Quinn Grundy, and Lisa A. Bero,
     "The Influence of Industry Sponsorship on the Research Agenda: A
     Scoping Review," *American Journal of Public Health*. 2018. 108(11):
     e9-e16. doi: 10.2105/AJPH.2018.304677, https://www.ncbi.nlm.
     nih.gov/pmc/articles/PMC6187765/

210 Justin E. Bekelman, Yan Li, and Cary P. Gross, "Scope and Impact
     of Financial Conflicts of Interest on Biomedical Research: A

Systematic Review," *JAMA*. 2003. 289(4): 454–465. doi: 10.1001/jama.289.4.454. PMID: 12533125, https://pubmed.ncbi.nlm.nih.gov/12533125/

211 Shelley Wood, "The Price of Knowledge: Industry-Sponsored Studies in the Era of Evidence-Based Medicine," *tctMD*, 27 September 2024, https://www.tctmd.com/news/price-knowledge-industry-sponsored-studies-era-evidence-based-medicine

212 Amy Westervelt, "Fossil Fuel Companies Donated $700m to US Universities Over 10 Years," *The Guardian*, 1 March 2023, https://www.theguardian.com/environment/2023/mar/01/fossil-fuel-companies-donate-millions-us-universities

213 Ruth A. Brenner, Gitanjali Saluja Taneja, Denise L. Haynie, Ann C. Trumble, Cong Qian, Ron M. Klinger et al., "Association Between Swimming Lessons and Drowning in Childhood: A Case-Control Study," *Archives of Pediatrics and Adolescent Medicine*. 2009. 163(3): 203–210. doi:10.1001/archpediatrics.2008.563, https://jamanetwork.com/journals/jamapediatrics/fullarticle/381058; Justin Scarr, "Floods Highlight Deeper Problem of Childhood Drowning in Asia," *International Life Saving Federation*, 28 October 2011, https://www.ilsf.org/2011/10/28/media-release-floods-highlight-deeper-problem-of-childhood-drowning-in-asia/

214 See https://www.savethechildren.org

215 See https://www.heifer.org

216 Anthony Capretto, "How a Sports Car and SUV Saved Porsche from Bankruptcy," *CarBuzz*, 24 August 2024, https://carbuzz.com/boxster-or-cayenne-save-porsche-bankruptcy/

217 Stephanie Strom, "With Tastes Growing Healthier, McDonald's Aims to Adapt Its Menu," *New York Times*, 26 September 2013, https://www.nytimes.com/2013/09/27/business/mcdonalds-moves-toward-a-healthier-menu.html

218 Jason Stein, "Marketing: Eddie Bauer Helped Ford Start a SUV Giant," *Automotive News*, 27 October 2003, https://www.autonews.com/article/20031027/REG/310270707/

marketing-eddie-bauer-helped-ford-start-an-suv-giant

219 Jeremy Riggall, "The Black Mambas: South Africa's All-Female Anti-Poaching Unit," *BBC*, 21 November 2023, https://www.bbc.com/future/article/20231120-the-black-mambas-south-africas-all-female-anti-poaching-unit

220 Joe Cochrane, "Indonesia's Forest Fires Take Toll on Wildlife, Big and Small," *New York Times*, 30 October 2015, https://www.nytimes.com/2015/10/31/world/asia/indonesia-forest-fires-wildlife.html; Ben Otto, "Businesses Take Heat from Haze in Indonesia," *Wall Street Journal*, 3 November 2015, https://www.wsj.com/articles/businesses-take-heat-from-haze-in-indonesia-1446554641; Trisha Mukherjee, "Out of Control Fires Rage the Amazon Region," *ABC News*, 10 September 2024, https://abcnews.go.com/International/control-fires-ravage-amazon-region/story?id=113545475; see also https://earthobservatory.nasa.gov/global-maps/MOD14A1_M_FIRE

221 Jody Greene, "Why Failure is so Important to Success," *Forbes*, 12 November 2012, https://www.forbes.com/sites/chicceo/2012/10/31/why-failure-is-so-important-to-success/; Mike Herd, "Why Failure is an Important Part of Success on Business," *Small Business*, 29 May 2015, https://smallbusiness.co.uk/why-failure-is-an-important-part-of-success-in-business-2485866/; Julian Birkinshaw and Martine Haas, "Increase Your Return on Failure," *Harvard Business Review*, May 2016, https://hbr.org/2016/05/increase-your-return-on-failure/

222 Frank L. Dyer and Thomas C. Martin, *Edison: His Life and Invention* (New York and London: Harper & Brothers, 1910), ch. 24, https://gutenberg.org/files/820/820-h/820-h.htm

223 See https://www.biography.com/inventors/thomas-edison; https://www.history.com/topics/inventions/thomas-edison

224 See https://thomasedison.org/edison-quotes

225 Grant Ennis, *Dark PR: How Corporate Disinformation Harms Undermines Our Health and the Environment*, (Cantley, QC: Daraja Press, 2023).

226 Richard G. Frank, Leslie Dach, and Nicole Lurie, "It Was the Government That Produced COVID-19 Vaccine Success," *Health Affairs*, 14 May 2021, https://www.healthaffairs.org/content/forefront/government-produced-covid-19-vaccine-success; Jennifer Kates, Cynthia Cox, and Josh Michaud, "How Much Could COVID-19 Vaccines Cost the U.S. After Commercialization?" *KFF*, 10 March 2023, https://www.kff.org/coronavirus-covid-19/issue-brief/how-much-could-covid-19-vaccines-cost-the-u-s-after-commercialization/

227 Hussain S. Lalani, Jerry Avorn, and Aaron S. Kesselheim, "US Taxpayers Heavily Funded the Discovery of COVID-19 Vaccines," *Clinical Pharmacology & Therapeutics*. 2022. 111(3): 542–544. doi: 10.1002/cpt.2344, https://www.ncbi.nlm.nih.gov/pmc/articles/PMC8426978/

228 Esther de Haan, "Big Pharma Raked in USD 90 Billion in Profits with COVID-19 Vaccines," *SOMO*, 27 February 2023, https://www.somo.nl/big-pharma-raked-in-usd-90-billion-in-profits-with-covid-19-vaccines

229 Joachim Hagopian, "Death and Extinction of the Bees: The Role of Monsanto?" *Centre for Research on Globalization*, 28 March 2014, https://www.globalresearch.ca/death-and-extinction-of-the-bees/5375684

230 UN Environment Programme, "Why Bees Are Essential to People and Planet," 18 May 2022, https://www.unep.org/news-and-stories/story/why-bees-are-essential-people-and-planet

231 Irina Panțiru, Amy Ronaldson, Nicusor F. Sima and A. Dregan, "The Impact of Gardening on Well-Being, Mental Health, and Quality of Life: An Umbrella Review and Meta-Analysis," *Systematic Reviews*. 2024. 13(1): 45. https://doi.org/10.1186/s13643-024-02457-9, https://systematicreviewsjournal.biomedcentral.com/articles/10.1186/s13643-024-02457-9

232 "30 Tips for Increasing Your Home's Value," *HGTV*, website accessed 30 September 2024, https://www.hgtv.com/design/

remodel/interior-remodel/30-tips-for-increasing-your-homes-value

233 S. N., "How Do Bike-Sharing Schemes Shape Cities?" *The Economist*, 23 October 2013, https://www.economist.com/the-economist-explains/2013/10/22/how-do-bike-sharing-schemes-shape-cities

234 Peter Walker, "Segregated Cycle Superhighways Set for Go-Ahead in London," *The Guardian*, 4 February 2015, https://www.theguardian.com/uk-news/2015/feb/04/segregated-cycle-lanes-london-tfl

235 Liz Thomas, "Public Attitudes Towards Bike-Sharing," *Yale Environment Review*, 17 March 2014, https://environment-review.yale.edu/public-attitudes-towards-bike-sharing-0

236 See https://www.youtube.com/watch?v=mc_IgE7TBSY

237 National Museum of American Diplomacy, "Tie a Yellow Ribbon: The Origin of the National Response to the Iran Hostage Crisis," 19 January 2021, https://diplomacy.state.gov/stories/yellow-ribbon-hostages/

238 Jennifer Yurchisin, Yoo Jin Kwon, and Sara Marcketti, "Consumers of Charity Bracelets: Cause-Supporters or Fashion-Followers?" *Journal of Fashion Marketing and Management*. 2009. 13: 448–457, doi:10.1108/13612020910974546, https://dr.lib.iastate.edu/entities/publication/3e473f99-7a26-4b8d-9185-656a0916a709

239 See https://smokeybear.com

240 See https://wwf.panda.org/discover/knowledge_hub/endangered_species/giant_panda

241 Maria Cohn and Morgen Bromell, "The 50 Most Iconic Brand Logos of All Time," *Complex*, 7 March 2013, https://www.complex.com/life/a/maria-cohn/the-50-most-iconic-brand-logos-of-all-time

242 See https://www.komen.org

243 See https://www.autismspeaks.org

244 See https://www.toysfortots.org

245 See https://www.wlsl.org

246 See https://www.daisydash5k.com

247 Andrew Chamberlain, "What Matters More to Your Workforce Than Money," *Harvard Business Review*, 17 January 2017, https://hbr.org/2017/01/what-matters-more-to-your-workforce-than-money

248 See https://www.opm.gov/policy-data-oversight/performance-management/reference-materials/historical/benefits-of-using-nonmonetary-awards

249 Johns Hopkins University, "The Changing Generational Values," 17 November 2022, https://imagine.jhu.edu/blog/2022/11/17/the-changing-generational-values

250 Issie Lapowsky, "10 Things Employees Want Most," *Inc.*, 27 August 2010, https://www.inc.com/guides/2010/08/10-things-employees-want.html

CHAPTER 9

251 See https://quoteinvestigator.com/2017/11/12/change-world/

252 "Communication," *Merriam-Webster Dictionary*, https://www.merriam-webster.com/dictionary/communication

253 George A. Miller, "The Magical Number Seven, Plus or Minus Two: Some Limits on Our Capacity for Processing Information,"cc *Psychological Review.* 1956. 63(2): 81–97. doi: 10.1037/h0043156

254 See https://debatrix.com/en/2023/04/17/why-number-7-2-is-a-magic-number-in-your-brain/

255 Suzanne B. Shu and Kurt A. Carlson, "When Three Charms but Four Alarms: Identifying the Optimal Number of Claims in Persuasion Settings," *UCLA Anderson School of Management*, 2007, https://www.anderson.ucla.edu/faculty/suzanne.shu/Shu Carlson Three in Persuasion.pdf

256 Microsoft, *Attention Spans: Consumer Insights, Microsoft Canada*, spring 2015, https://dl.motamem.org/microsoft-attention-spans-research-report.pdf

257 See https://www.roadtrafficsigns.com/traffic-sign-universal-language

258 Adriana Galvan, Todd A. Hare, Henning U. Voss, Gary Glover,

and B. J. Casey, "Risk-Taking and the Adolescent Brain: Who is at Risk?" *Developmental Science*, 2007. 10(2): F8–F14. doi: 10:1111/j.1467-7687.2006.0579.x; B. J. Casey, Rebecca M. Jones, and Todd A. Hare, "The Adolescent Brain," *Annals of the New York Academy of Sciences*. 2008. 1124: 111–126. doi: 10.1196/annals.1440.010, http://www.ncbi.nlm.nih.gov/pmc/articles/PMC2475802/

259 Oleksandra Mamchii, "Top 10 Most Powerful Men in the World in 2024," *Best Diplomats*, 22 January 2024, https://bestdiplomats.org/most-powerful-men-in-the-world/; see also https://time.com/collection/100-most-influential-people-2024/

260 Karen Valley, "Malala Strikes Back: Behind the Scenes of Her Fearless, Fast-Growing Organization," *Fast Company*, 18 November 2015, https://www.fastcompany.com/3052875/malala-strikes-back-behind-the-scenes-of-her-fearless-organization

261 MADD, "Candace Lightner," 24 September 1980, https://madd.org/history/candace-lightner/

262 See https://www.eeoc.gov/laws/guidance/equal-pay-act-1963-and-lilly-ledbetter-fair-pay-act-2009

263 See https://drowningpreventionfoundation.org/board/

264 The Sentry, "Not On Our Watch and The Sentry Have Merged," 20 March 2019, https://thesentry.org/2019/03/20/2498/not-watch-sentry-merged/

265 See https://www.unicef.org/serbia/en/partnerships-and-ambassadors

266 See https://www.headstogether.org.uk/

267 See https://www.fondationprincessecharlene.mc/en

268 Paola Gianturco, *Grandmother Power: A Global Phenomenon* (Brooklyn, NY: powerHouse Books, 2012).

269 We met at the World Conference on Drowning Prevention in Danang, Vietnam in 2011.

270 Ernesto Ruiz-Tiben and Donald R. Hopkins, "Dracunculiasis (Guinea Worm Disease) Eradication," Advances in Parasitology.

2006. 61: 275–309. doi: 10.1016/S0065-308X(05)61007-X, https://pubmed.ncbi.nlm.nih.gov/16735167/; Carter Center, "Guinea Worm Eradication Program. Update 14: Human Cases of Guinea Worm Reported in 2023," 6 March 2024, https://www.cartercenter.org/health/guinea_worm/index.html

271 Cedars-Sinai Hospital, "Is Dry Drowning a Real Danger to Your Children?" 18 July 2019, https://www.cedars-sinai.org/newsroom/is-dry-drowning-a-real-danger-to-your-children/

272 See https://www.hsph.harvard.edu/chc/harvard-alcohol-project; Howard Koh and Pamela Yatsko, "Jay Winsten and the Designated Driver Campaign," Harvard Business School Case Study, February 2017, #ALI013-PDF-ENG, https://www.hsph.harvard.edu/chc/2017/02/01/jay-winsten-and-the-designated-driver-campaign/

273 Stacy Jo Dixon, "Facebook: Quarterly Number of MAU (Monthly Active Users) Worldwide 2008–2023," *Statista*, 21 May 2024, https://www.statista.com/statistics/264810/number-of-monthly-active-facebook-users-worldwide/

274 Mansour Iqbal, "Twitter Revenue and Usage Statistics (2024)," *Business of Apps*, 22 February 2024, https://www.businessofapps.com/data/twitter-statistics/; Oskar Mortensen, "How Many Users on Instagram? Statistics & Facts (2024)," *SEO.AI*, 24 April 2024, https://seo.ai/blog/how-many-users-on-instagram

275 Lewis Ogden, "30 Eye-Opening YouTube Facts, Figures and Statistics You Should Know in 2024," *CloudIncome*, 23 February 2024, https://cloudincome.com/youtube-statistics/; Shubham Singh, "How Many People Use YouTube (2024 Statistics)," *DemandSage*, 14 August 2024, https://www.demandsage.com/youtube-stats/

276 See https://www.youtube.com/watch?v=IJNR2EpS0jw

277 The official video now requires approved access. A bootleg is available at https://www.youtube.com/watch?v=z1A5BtqsaP

278 See https://www.youtube.com/watch?v=pZwvrxVavnQ

279 Lee V. Gaines and Nicole Cohen, "Just Say No Didn't Actually

Protect Students from Drugs. Here's What Could," *NPR,* 19 December 2023, https://www.npr.org/2023/11/09/1211217460/ fentanyl-drug-education-dare

280 See https://www.earthhour.org/about/the-biggest-hour-for-earth

281 See https://www.heforshe.org/en

282 See https://iknowpolitics.org/en/learn/video/ emma-watson-introduces-new-heforsheorg

283 Ruth Reichl, *Tender at the Bone: Growing Up at the Table* (London: Random House, 1998), pp. 258–259.

284 Roger Biles, "Machine Politics," *Encyclopedia of Chicago,* 2005, http://www.encyclopedia.chicagohistory.org/pages/774.html

285 See https://www.toms.com/en-us/impact/report

CHAPTER 10

286 Leo Tolstoy, "Three Methods of Reform." *In Pamphlets: Translated from the Russian*, tr. Aylmer Maude (Christchurch: Free Age Press, 1900), p. 29.

287 "Behavior," Merriam-Webster Dictionary, https://www.merriam-webster.com/dictionary/behavior

288 "Habit," Merriam-Webster Dictionary, https://www.merriam-webster.com/dictionary/habit

289 Committee on Fostering Healthy Mental, Emotional, and Behavioral Development Among Children and Youth, "Influences on Mental, Emotional, and Behavioral Development." In *Fostering Healthy Mental, Emotional, and Behavioral Development in Children and Youth: A National Agenda. A Consensus Study Report of the National Academies of Sciences, Engineering, and Medicine* (Washington, DC: National Academies Press, 2019), ch. 2, https://www.ncbi.nlm.nih.gov/books/NBK551846

290 Laurence Steinberg and Kathryn C. Monahan, "Age Differences in Resistance to Peer Influence," *Developmental Psychology.* 2007. 43(6): 1531–1543. doi: 10.1037/0012-1649.43.6.1531, https://www.ncbi.nlm.nih.gov/pmc/articles/PMC2779518/; Lisa J. Knoll, Jovita

T. Leung, Lucy Foulkes, and Sarah-Jayne Blakemore, "Age-Related Differences in Social Influence on Risk Perception Depend on the Direction of Influence," *Journal of Adolescence*. 2017. 60: 53–63. doi: 10.1016/j.adolescence.2017.07.002, https://www.ncbi.nlm.nih.gov/pmc/articles/PMC5614112/

291 Harvard Medical School, "Why It's Hard to Change Unhealthy Behavior – And Why You Should Keep Trying," 20 July 2021, https://www.health.harvard.edu/mind-and-mood/why-its-hard-to-change-unhealthy-behavior-and-why-you-should-keep-trying

292 Phillippa Lally, Cornelia H. M. van Jaarsveld, Henry W. W. Potts, and Jane Wardle, "How Are Habits Formed: Modeling Habit Formation in the Real World," *European Journal of Social Psychology*. 2010. 40(6): 998–1009, https://onlinelibrary.wiley.com/doi/abs/10.1002/ejsp.674

293 Neil A. Bradbury, "Attention Span During Lectures, 8 Seconds, 10 Minutes, or More?" *Advances in Physiology Education*. 2016. 40: 509–513. doi: 10.1152/advan.00109.2016, https://journals.physiology.org/doi/pdf/10.1152/advan.00109.2016

294 Philipp Lorenz-Spreen, Bjarke Mørche Mønsted, Philipp Hövel, and Sune Lehmann, "Accelerating Dynamics of Collective Attention," *Nature Communications*. 2019. 10: 1759. https://doi.org/10.1038/s41467-019-09311-w, https://www.nature.com/articles/s41467-019-09311-w

295 Saul McLeod, "Operant Conditioning: What It Is, How It Works, and Examples," *Simply Psychology*, updated 2 February 2024, https://www.simplypsychology.org/operant-conditioning.html

296 Institute of Medicine and National Research Council Committee on the Science of Adolescence, *The Science of Adolescent Risk-Taking: Workshop Report* (Washington, DC: National Academies Press, 2011), ch. 3; American Academy of Child & Adolescent Psychiatry, "Teen Brain: Behavior, Problem Solving, and Decision Making," No. 95, September 2017, https://www.aacap.org/AACAP/Families_and_Youth/Facts_for_Families/FFF-Guide/

The-Teen-Brain-Behavior-Problem-Solving-and-Decision-Making-095.aspx

297 Jill Bolte Taylor, "The Neuroanatomical Transformation of the Teenage Brain: Jill Bolte Taylor at TEDxYouth@Indianapolis," 21 February 2013, *YouTube*, https://www.youtube.com/watch?v=PzT_SBl31-s

298 Valerie Boon, "Why Danger is Exciting – But Only to Some People," *The Conversation*, 5 September 2016, https://theconversation.com/why-danger-is-exciting-but-only-to-some-people-64680; Bill Eddy, "How to Quickly Spot High-Conflict People," *Psychology Today*, 21 November 2021, https://www.psychologytoday.com/us/blog/5-types-of-people-who-can-ruin-your-life/201711/how-to-quickly-spot-high-conflict-people

299 Charles Stangor, Hammond Tarry, and Rajiv Jhangiani, "Changing Attitudes by Changing Behavior." In *Principles of Social Psychology: 1st International Edition* (2011), ch. 4.3, https://opentextbc.ca/socialpsychology/chapter/changing-attitudes-by-changing-behavior/

300 Ed Robinson, "Should We Pay Students for Good Grades?" *University of Chicago Booth School of Business*, 24 May 2016, https://www.chicagobooth.edu/review/should-we-pay-students-good-grades

301 University of Cambridge, "Harsh Discipline Increases Risk of Children Developing Lasting Mental Health Problems," 31 March 2023, https://www.cam.ac.uk/research/news/harsh-discipline-increases-risk-of-children-developing-lasting-mental-health-problems

302 Lydia Saad, "Americans Widely Support Tighter Regulations on Gun Sales," *Gallup*, 17 October 2017, https://news.gallup.com/poll/220637/americans-widely-support-tighter-regulations-gun-sales.aspx

303 Rebecca Hasdell, *What We Know About Universal Basic Income: A Cross-Synthesis of Reviews* (Stanford, CA: Basic Income Lab, 2020), https://basicincome.stanford.edu/uploads/Umbrella Review

BI_final.pdf

304 Stangor et al., "Attitudes, Behavior, and Persuasion," ch. 4, https://opentextbc.ca/socialpsychology/chapter/chapter-summary-4/

305 Saul McLeod, "What is Cognitive Dissonance Theory?" *Simply Psychology*, 24 October 2023, https://www.simplypsychology.org/cognitive-dissonance.html

306 Hiroko Tabuchi, "Worse Than Anyone Expected: Air Travel Emissions Vastly Outpace Predictions," *New York Times*, 20 September 2019, https://www.nytimes.com/2019/09/19/climate/air-travel-emissions.html

307 Henning Steinfeld, Food and Agriculture Organization of the United Nations, and Livestock, Environment and Development Initiative, *Livestock's Long Shadow: Environmental Issues and Options* (Geneva, FAO, 2006), p. xxi, https://openknowledge.fao.org/server/api/core/bitstreams/36ade937-4641-46ed-aac4-6162717d8a7f/content

308 Mark Zuckerberg, "Four Ideas to Regulate the Internet," *Meta*, 30 March 2019, https://about.fb.com/news/2019/03/four-ideas-regulate-internet

309 See https://alcoholjustice.org; Christopher Ingraham, "Think You Drink a Lot? This Chart Will Tell You," *Washington Post*, 25 September 2014, https://www.washingtonpost.com/news/wonk/wp/2014/09/25/think-you-drink-a-lot-this-chart-will-tell-you/

310 John P. Kotter and Leonard A. Schlesinger, "Choosing Strategies for Change," *Harvard Business Review*, March–April 1979. 57(2).

311 Eric Westervelt, "How Investing in Preschool Beats the Stock Market, Hands Down," *NPR*, 12 December 2016, https://www.npr.org/sections/ed/2016/12/12/504867570/how-investing-in-preschool-beats-the-stock-market-hands-down; see also https://www.impact.upenn.edu/early-childhood-toolkit/why-invest/what-is-the-return-on-investment

312 Richard Ingersoll, Lisa Merrill, and Daniel Stuckey, *Seven Trends: The Transformation of the Teaching Force* (Philadelphia, PA:

Consortium for Policy Research in Education, 2014), https://cpre.
org/sites/default/files/workingpapers/1506_7trendsapril2014.pdf

313 Renate Haas, *Gender and Language Learning* (Tübingen: Narr
Francke Attempto Verla, 2016), p. 48.

314 See https://psychology.iresearchnet.com/social-psychology/control/
behavioral-contagion

315 Mir M. Ali and Debra S. Dwyer, "Estimating Peer Effects
in Adolescent Smoking Behavior: A Longitudinal Analysis,"
Journal of Adolescent Health. 2009. 45(4): 402–408. doi:
10.1016/j.jadohealth.2009.02.004, https://pubmed.ncbi.nlm.nih.
gov/19766946/

316 Robert H. Frank, "Behavioral Contagion Could Spread the Benefits
of a Carbon Tax," *New York Times*, 19 August 2020, https://www.
nytimes.com/2020/08/19/business/behavioral-contagion-carbon-
tax.html

317 Robert Cass Keller, "We Must All Hang Together …" *Word Ways.*
1976. 9(1): 3, https://digitalcommons.butler.edu/wordways/vol9/
iss1/3/

CHAPTER 11

318 See https://fortune.com/2023/08/30/warren-buffett-best-quotes-
93-birthday-august-30-swimming-naked/

319 See https://www.britannica.com/biography/Sunzi

320 Sun Tzu, *The Art of War*, tr. Lionel Giles (Garsington: Benediction
Classics, 2018), https://classics.mit.edu/Tzu/artwar.html

321 Roger Fisher and William Ury, *Getting to Yes: Negotiating
Agreement Without Giving In* (Boston and New York: Houghton
Mifflin, 1981).

322 Taylor Landis, "Customer Retention Marketing vs.
Customer Acquisition Marketing," *Outbound Engine*,
12 April 2022, https://www.outboundengine.com/blog/
customer-retention-marketing-vs-customer-acquisition-marketing/

323 See https://www.firstthingsfirst.org/early-childhood-matters/

investing-in-early-childhood

324 Fazlur Rahman, Saideep Bose, Michael Linnan, Aminur Rahman, Saidur Mashreky, Benjamin Haaland, and Eric Finkelstein, "Cost-effectiveness of an Injury and Drowning Prevention Program in Bangladesh," *Pediatrics*. 2012. 130(6): e1621–1628. doi: 10.1542/peds.2012-0757, https://pubmed.ncbi.nlm.nih.gov/23147971/. Erratum in: Rahman et al., *Pediatrics*. 2020. 146(4): e2020021501. doi: 10.1542/peds.2020-021501. Correction in: *Pediatrics*. 2021. 147(6): e2021051078. doi: 10.1542/peds.2021-051078; see also https://nagerpoursurvivre.com/en/swim-to-survive/

325 Susanné Seong-eun Bergsten and Song Ah Lee, "The Global Backlash Against Women's Rights: A Stark Reminder on International Women's Day," *Human Rights Watch*, 7 March 2023, https://www.hrw.org/news/2023/03/07/global-backlash-against-womens-rights

326 "A letter from the Right Hon. Edmund Burke, M.P. in the kingdom of Great Britain, to Sir Hercules Langrishe: Bart. M.P. on the subject of Roman Catholics of Ireland, and the propriety of admitting them to the elective franchise, consistently with the principles of the constitution as established at the Revolution" (1792), *Eighteenth Century Collections Online*, University of Michigan Library Digital Collections, https://name.umdl.umich.edu/004804966.0001.000

ABOUT THE AUTHOR

Rebecca participated in her first protest march at the age of 10. An activist with a focus on helping the world's children, she most recently tackled the hidden global epidemic of drowning. Her focus is on changing attitudes and behaviors by integrating principles of social psychology, marketing, and business. Rebecca holds a B.A. in Finance from the University of Illinois, a Master's in Management concentrating on marketing, economics, and international management from the Kellogg School of Management at Northwestern University, and a Master's in Organizational and Social Psychology from the London School of Economics.

www.ingramcontent.com/pod-product-compliance
Lightning Source LLC
Chambersburg PA
CBHW061246120726
48001CB00001B/177